It's
HARD
Not to
HATE YOU

Also by Valerie Frankel

NOVELS

Four of a Kind

I Take This Man

Hex and the Single Girl

The Girlfriend Curse

The Not-So-Perfect Man

The Accidental Virgin

Smart Vs. Pretty

Fringe Girl

Fringe Girl in Love

American Fringe

Fringe Benefits

A Deadline for Murder

Murder on Wheels

Prime Time for Murder

A Body to Die For

NONFICTION

Thin Is the New Happy: A Memoir

Men Are Stupid and They Like Big Boobs: A Woman's Guide to Beauty Through Plastic Surgery (by Joan Rivers with V.F.)

The Best You'll Ever Have: What Every Woman Needs to Know About Getting and Giving Knock-Your-Socks-Off Sex (by Shannon Mullen with V.F.)

Prime-Time Style (with Ellen Tien)

The I Hate My Job Handbook (with Ellen Tien)

The Heartbreak Handbook (with Ellen Tien)

It's
HARD
Not to
HATE YOU

....

Valerie Frankel

St. Martin's Press

New York

ISBN 978-0-312-60978-8

First Edition: September 2011

10 9 8 7 6 5 4 3 2 1

Dedicated to:
My Amazing Lifers
(You Know Who You Are)

CONTENTS

It's
HARD
Not to
HATE YOU

One

·················

Hate Happens

I might've broken the official Guinness World Record for longest sulk in history. It started at 3:30 PM on Friday, as soon as I stepped off the schoolbus on the corner by my house in Short Hills, New Jersey. I dragged myself home and sank into the couch in what we called the den. The epic mope continued, unabated, until Sunday afternoon.

"Why don't you call someone?" asked Judy, my mom.

She didn't know that I had attempted to scrounge up plans.

"Hello, Mrs. Allen," I said when I'd called. "It's Valerie. Is Amy there?"

Muffled sound of the mouthpiece being palmed. Then Amy's mom came back on the line. "I'm sorry, she's at her cousin's in Connecticut for the weekend."

"Hello, Mrs. Bernstein," I tried next. "Is Brenda there?"

"One second," she said. The white noise of being put on hold filled my ear. Then, crackle, she came back on the line and said, "Sorry, Brenda went to the movies with her dad."

I could almost see Brenda standing next to her mother, nodding approvingly while they conspired to lie to me. In all fairness, Amy and Brenda weren't really my "friends" anyway (anymore). Once, we'd pricked our fingers with a pin and declared ourselves blood sisters. But that was forever ago, back in sixth grade. We were in seventh grade now. Sixth-grade graduates from the five elementary schools across Short Hills and Millburn Township converged at the bigger, tougher junior high. Old loyalties suddenly irrelevant, the friendship deck was reshuffled. Amy and Brenda—skinny, cute, with shiny hair and clear skin—were among the queens of the new social strata.

I used to be cute. Then, the summer between sixth and seventh grade, my clear skin sprouted spots. My shiny hair frizzed. If I'd ever been slender, I was now plump. I saw the changes in the mirror, and hoped no one would notice. They did. Amy and Brenda, fearing contagion, took one look at me in September and froze me out. In the hallways, when I said hi, their eyes turned to glass. It was as if they'd never known me, like we hadn't spent countless sleepovers at each other's houses, mingled finger blood, and flashed our incoming pubic hair.

While twisting in the precarious social state of "between cliques," I hadn't yet convinced a new crew of like-minded teen misanthropes to take me in. Calling Amy and Brenda that Sunday was an act of masochistic desperation. But the only thing worse than being snubbed by girls who hated me was hanging around at home.

My epic sulk tableau—girl flung on a couch, arm draped

over face to hide the sorrow—didn't inspire Mom's pathos. If she'd had her way, I'd be dropping and giving her twenty, or on the exercise bike, or chased up a tree by wild dogs, anything that burned calories.

"What are Brenda and Amy doing today?" she asked, looking down at me on the couch.

As far as she knew, my social standing was the same as last year, when I'd been popular. I didn't dare tell her that my perilous fall from grace had been like stepping off the Empire State Building blindfolded. I'd have sooner appeared on the cover of *Seventeen* magazine than tell Mom how right she was, that being ten pounds overweight had made me lonely and miserable, just as she predicted. Mom had been sounding the alarm for a while already, putting me on diets, weighing me weekly, yelling when I stole into the pantry for junk food that my scrawny older sister and athletic younger brother could scarf at will.

Even in her bleakest visions, Mom couldn't have dreamed just how bad things were for me at school. Not only had I been rendered invisible by my former friends, but a cabal of boys had chosen me as their favorite target of abuse. They circled me in the halls, knocked my books to the floor, snarled "beast" in my face. They oinked and mooed at my back. The bus trip to and from school? A hell ride of ridicule during which one or two boys could rally thirty kids to chant "pig" at me in unison. I swear sometimes the bus driver joined in. No wonder Amy and Brenda had dumped me. Associating with me would be a case of beast by association.

"I can't take another minute of you sulking on the couch,"

said Mom, her impatience escalating by the minute. "Do something! Go run around the block." When Mom reached the apex of frustration and flew into a rage that would have her screaming and crying for hours, my dad, Howie, called her Judy Black. By Sunday afternoon, two full days into my mope, Mom had reached Judy Gray levels. And the storm clouds were darkening.

"What's this?" she asked, spotting the cellophane wrapper of a Twinkie I'd stashed under a couch pillow. Crinkling it in her hand, she said, "Is this what you've been doing all day? Sneaking food?"

For her information, I had been very busy, actually, attending to important matters. If only steamy fantasizing melted fat. In my mind, adorable Carlo had been slipping his hot pink tongue between my parted lips for hours. Carlo was a new kid at school, still an outsider. Despite his golden nimbus of curls, his long tan legs and dimples, he was, like me, in need of friends. Maybe he hadn't sorted out yet that I was a total pariah. Or, if he had, maybe he'd see beyond the Godzilla label and notice *me*, maybe like-like me, or even better, French kiss the bejeez out of me.

It was lust at first sight—and a geographically convenient one at that. I'd seen the moving truck in front of the white house at the end of my block in late August. Carlo appeared on the street on his ten-speed later, like Apollo on a sun chariot, riding to New Jersey to choose a mortal mate. Even though I'd barely spoken to him, I felt a rightful claim. Carlo lived so close. He'd practically been delivered to my doorstep. He was my reward, a taste of bliss to counterbalance the steady diet of humiliation I dealt with at school, and at home from Mom.

With a heroic grunt, I got off the couch. Mom asked, "Where are you going?"

"For a jog," I announced. All the way to Carlo's house. Maybe he'd be hanging around outside. Maybe he'd wave at me. I'd stop to say hello, and we could have an actual conversation. Maybe he'd invite me in for a Tab. Or whatever.

I changed into my tube socks with three bar stripes, navy gym shorts with white piping along the sides, a T-shirt from the Club Med in Guadalupe where my family had gone on vacation, and a pair of Pumas. In the late 1970s, America had fallen passionately in love with running. Alas, the innovators at Nike had not yet invented a sports bra. I was already stacked, so I could have used the support. Where Carlo was concerned, I thought my bust would be a boon. I imagined him ogling me as I ran toward him on the street, my feathered wings and boobs bouncing in sync, braces gleaming in the afternoon sun, his eyes popping, jaw dropping with dumb desire.

I hit the road, and was winded and gasping within half a block. But still, I pushed on. Dad, a Jim Fixx devotee, told me that running-related pain could be overcome. "It's mind over matter," he said. "If you focus, you can train yourself to ignore the pain, or pretend it isn't there."

Rounding the bend, I could see the post-and-rail fence that enclosed Carlo's yard. I sensed him before I saw him. Just as I'd hoped, he was outside, sitting on the fence, his long legs dangling temptingly. But he wasn't alone. Two girls were with him. Their three heads turned in my direction. Amy was on the fence to his right. Brenda sat on his left. Apparently, they were not in Connecticut or at the movies, but together, at the house of the beautiful boy who'd arrived via golden chariot to my doorstep. A hitch in my bouncing breast, I realized with defeat that I hadn't been the only girl at school to notice Carlo's blond lanky dimpled adorableness.

They'd seen me. I couldn't turn back, run home, and hide. I had to keep moving forward. The adrenaline rush of seeing Carlo, and then the flood of cortisol—the fight-or-flight hormone—upon seeing Amy and Brenda, fired my pace to double time. Since I couldn't get away fast enough, I needed the speed, which, granted, was a relative crawl.

Feeling their eyes on me, I clenched my stomach muscles and wished I could hold my boobs to keep them from flopping. Carlo cupped his hands around his mouth and yelled at me, "Keep running!" The peal of Amy and Brenda's laughter rang in my ears—red hot with mortification—far longer than I could actually hear it.

Huffing and puffing, I made a loop on the next block and ran straight home, up the stairs, and into my room. Mom was there, sitting on my bed, a pile of Hostess wrappers—some of them weeks old—on my blanket. I'd been outside for all of ten minutes. She must have come up to my room the second I left and begun her search. She'd found my detritus quickly. Not gifted (yet) at subterfuge, I'd merely crammed the wrappers into the back corner of my desk drawer.

She was crying, in Judy Black mode. "Why are you doing this to me?" she asked, crinkling the wrappers. Mom believed my weight was her problem, and that my stealing food was a crime I perpetrated against her. The truth? It totally was. I was a spiteful little sprite, every bite was a fuck-you aimed at her. But I still didn't want to get caught! That would mean a marathon session of accusations, ranting, raving, with Mom asking, "Do you want to be fat and miserable your whole life?"

Which was exactly what I got. All the while, I stood there in my shorts and tube socks staring at the daisy-shaped rug on the floor. When she finally left, I barricaded my bedroom door with a wicker armchair loaded down with stuffed animals. The door had no lock, sadly. I was terrified she'd barge back in (". . . and another thing!") to serve me a second helping. I could hear her crying downstairs in the kitchen. Dad was comforting her, assuring her that she was a good mother. He would have said anything—and often did—to get her to stop crying. Managing Mom's erratic emotions was a big job. Dad quickly ran out of comforting words, none left over for me.

I sat at my desk and found my red corduroy journal in the top drawer, right next to where the wrappers had been wedged. Instead of rummaging for trash, Mom could have opened the journal. If she had, she'd have known *exactly* how much I appreciated her efforts to make me thinner/happier.

As an adolescent diarist, my anger was too raw and intense to own (in an Oprah sense), so I filtered the hate through an alter-ego character named Sal. She was the author of gloomy free-verse poetry and first-person howls of throbbing black angst. Lately Sal had branched out into third-person narrative, curdling stories of revenge against the boys who teased her and the girls who laughed along. Sal was bloodthirsty and savage. Nemeses were decapitated, defenestrated, eaten by zombies, vaporized by toilet bombs.

Just now, while sprinting home, I had plotted Sal's revenge against Carlo. A massive sinkhole opened directly beneath his post-and-rail fence, swallowing him, along with poor, unlucky

Amy and Brenda (they picked the wrong day to lie about being in Connecticut and at the movies). In her togs, Sal jogged to the crumbling edge of the hole and peered down to see the three of them clinging to exposed tree roots, screaming and begging for help. Sal fed a rope down to them, yard after yard, still out of their reach, until—oops!—the end slipped through her fingers. She watched it shimmy into the pit of endless darkness, cupped her hands around her mouth, and hollered, "Sorry about that . . . that . . . that . . . that . . ." The apology echoed and faded, just like Carlo, Amy, and Brenda's futile cries for help.

Heh. The tale of vengeance had put wings on my Pumas for the loop home. But when I took out my journal to write it down, I was inspired to draw a self-portrait instead. I studied my reflection in the mirror that hung on the wall in front of my desk and put ballpoint Bic to paper.

I drew a reasonable likeness, with the center-part hairstyle, oval face, braces, and spots. One eye was Picasso-esque, larger and lower than the other. My nose was just an open triangle. The lips tight and straight. I would not be winning any junior artist awards, for sure. But I managed to capture a striking blankness, a void of emotional expression. The flat, intentionally two-dimensional quality represented my new ideal, a goal, the face I vowed to show the world from that day forward.

Mind over matter. I would train myself to ignore the pain and/or pretend it didn't exist. That was, it seemed to me, the only way I could possibly lurch forward, take another single step. If, by force of will, I could somehow hide my hurt and anger from those who inflamed it, if I showed no weakness, I'd win. I'd best them all.

Mom, and her constant criticism.

Dad, for not defending me and giving all his attention to Mom.

My sister, for being thin and perfect.

My brother, for being my mom's obvious favorite.

The boys who tormented me.

The girls who rejected me.

None of them would ever know how deeply their words and actions cut. They'd never see me wince. I'd show nothing but blank ambiguity. My enemies would wonder, "Does she even care?" while I secretly wished them dead and dismembered. Years before Lady Gaga was born, I designed a poker face—cockeyed and two-dimensional—that would be my shield, protecting and preserving my dignity, which was all I thought I had left.

I made that vow as an adolescent in an emotional crisis. Upholding it for decades wasn't the brightest idea. But secreting my anger and hate became habitual, natural. I was good at it, too, and prided myself on being, for the most part, unflappable. That drawing was the foundation upon which I built my identity. I would be the girl, and then the woman, who played it cool.

I captioned the portrait, "Me, 12."

During a recent bout of insomnia, I caught Woody Allen's *Manhattan* on late-night cable and laughed at his classic line, "I can't express anger. That's my problem. I internalize everything. I just grow a tumor instead."

My psychic friend Mary T. Browne would probably say

that it was no coincidence I happened to turn on the TV that night, at that hour, to that channel, to catch that line. It was prescient, to say the least.

My dad, Howie, a retired nephrologist, got tough with me in mid-April of 2009, telling me that I'd put off a colonoscopy for long enough. I was forty-four. He'd just had his every-five-year probe, which had yielded a precancerous polyp. Since his mother, and my grandmother, Edith Frankel, suffered four bouts of cancer in her life—including two colon cancers—Dad had been urging me for years to get my ass to a gastroenterologist. In a spring-cleaning fit of appointment making, I scheduled the screening.

Let me just say, my colonoscopy was a joy from beginning to end (as it were). The day before, I couldn't eat. In lieu of food, I had to down a gallon of "Nu-Litely," a sodium-flavored liquid best choked down with one hand holding the nose. This salty beverage made me "go," a polite euphemism. (Ladies don't like to type the words *shit* and *storm*.) The instructions were to chug eight ounces of Nu-Litely every ten minutes for three hours, which had me going, and going, all night long.

When I arrived at the hospital for the procedure, I was instructed to leave a urine sample, which they would test for pregnancy. But I couldn't. The Nu-Litely had completely dehydrated me. The anesthesiologist refused to treat me unless I squeezed out a few drops. See, if a pregnant woman receives a dose of the knockout drug Propofol, the growing fetus is in danger of turning into Michael Jackson. God forbid. I swore I was not pregnant. My husband, Steve, had had a vasectomy a few months before. The anesthesiologist didn't care if he'd had his dick cut clean off. If I couldn't pee in a cup, she said, the colonoscopy was off.

It was hard not to hate her. She was holding up the doctor's schedule and compounding my anxiety. I spent an hour in the restroom in my paper gown, my finger under warm water, thinking of babbling brooks and trickling streams. The nurses hooked me up to an IV with a saline drip. Three pints later, no go. I was so self-conscious about not being able to pee ("never seen this before," remarked a few of the nurses), my fear of the procedure, and what might be found that I'd put an emotional block on my bladder.

Luckily, the day before the procedure, I'd had some pretesting. According to the nurse's notes—which took an hour to locate—yesterday's preggers test had been negative. The anesthesiologist reluctantly agreed to proceed. Then she demanded to know if I'd done anything that could have resulted in a pregnancy the night before, when I'd been sequestered in the bathroom, weeping softly, for eight hours.

I'd already *told* her that Steve was shooting blanks. But I said, "My husband is very turned on by explosive diarrhea. Somehow, even in my weakened state, I managed to fend him off."

To shut me up, she injected the Propofol, which was blissfully effective. I could see what Michael Jackson loved about it. I was *out*. I woke up later to see my mom standing next to my bed in the recovery room, the nurses telling her the hilarious story of my not being able to pee in a cup. Of course, as soon as I heard that, I felt every drop of the three pints of liquid they'd pumped into my blood. I slurred that I needed the bathroom immediately (because I hadn't seen enough of a toilet in the last thirty hours).

Mom had come to Brooklyn Heights—where I lived, and had the procedure—from Short Hills to escort me home from the hospital. Steve couldn't be there himself, because he had to watch Lucy, our younger daughter, ten, at the annual May Day spring dance at her school. I'd been going to May Day dances since our older daughter Maggie, thirteen, was in preschool. This was the first one I'd missed in ten years. The first time I'd missed any school recital, concert, game, or dance.

Nice guy, the doctor. Mid-fifties, Jewish. He greeted Mom and me formally, as if he hadn't just snaked a camera up my rear. "I found and removed a three-centimeter polyp," he said, "from your sigmoid rectum [!!]. It's already been sent down to the lab. Our pathologists will look at it and have a report in a couple of weeks. I can give you color pictures of it, too, if you'd like."

"Lovely addition to any family album," I said, still a bit groggy from the drugs.

Mom, always quick to assume the worst, asked him, "What was your initial reaction when you saw the polyp? Did you think it was a tumor?"

"I really can't say," he said. "It was flat, took some time to get it all. Just be glad it's out. You told me that your paternal grandmother had early-onset uterine cancer and two colon cancers, correct?" Mom and I nodded. "And your father recently had a precancerous polyp removed?" Mom and I nodded again. "We should test your polyp for Lynch syndrome markers," he said.

Lynch syndrome. It was an easy name to remember. After Googling, I quickly learned that Lynch syndrome was a genetic mutation of proteins that killed abnormal cells in the colon, rectum, bladder, ureter, uterus, ovaries, pancreas, brain, and several other organs. If my family turned out to have the aptly named syndrome, my likelihood of getting one or more of these cancers was sky-high.

I also learned—a little Google could be a dangerous thing—that "flat" polyps, like mine, were more likely to be cancerous than not. I wouldn't know for sure until the pathology report came in.

The very next day after my anal intrusion, I went to the gynecologist to have a hysteroscopy—or a camera inserted through my cervix for a sightseeing tour of my uterus, another high-risk organ for Lynch syndrome. Two scopes in two days. I learned a lot—mainly, that all my secret places were sprouting growths.

The doctor inserted the scope, and I watched the postcards from my womb appear on the computer monitor next to the exam-room table. "What is *that?*" I asked, pointing at what looked like a flesh-colored stalactite.

My doctor—nice guy, mid-fifties, Jewish—said, "Good eye. It's a polyp. Oh, look at that. Wow! There's a whole *nest* of them! Let's get some pictures . . ."

I turned white. The nurse asked me if I was okay. I wondered if anyone had ever fainted with a camera in her vag before.

My gyn scheduled a procedure to have my uterus scraped clean of bumps, which took place less than a week after the colonoscopy, in the hospital operating room under anesthesia (more Propofol, yay!). Before *that* procedure, I had no problem peeing into a cup.

I could expect both pathology reports around the same time. It'd be another week of waiting and worrying.

Friends told me to be optimistic.

My attitude, though, was completely irrelevant to the outcome. My tissue samples were on a slide in some lab. Wishing and hoping would not magically alter their cellular structure. The polyps contained either normal or abnormal cells. If I cried myself to sleep every night, or watched *Zoolander* 24/7, it wouldn't matter. I resolved to ignore the scary situation until the results were in. But the strategy backfired. In a famous psych study from the 1980s, a shrink asked a group of subjects to ring a buzzer every time they thought of a white bear. He asked a second group of people *not* to think about a white bear, and ring the buzzer if they did anyway. Which group rang the buzzer twice as often? The "don't think bear" group.

I was a "don't think polyp" subject group of one. Despite my resolve, my thoughts returned to the image I saw on the computer screen. The gynecologist's comment—"Oh, wow, a whole nest of them"—echoed in my ears.

It bears mentioning that I had previous experience waiting for pathology reports and grim doctors delivering bad news. My first husband, Glenn, Maggie and Lucy's birth father, died of cancer nine years ago, when he was thirty-four. Our season in hell began in June 2000 with a sharp pain in Glenn's back that wouldn't go away. He had an MRI that revealed metastases along his spine, multiple brain lesions, and the primary tumor in his lung. After five months of ineffective treatment, he died in November 2000. I became a thirty-five-year-old widow with two young kids. Lucy was still in diapers; Maggie, a kindergartener.

Glenn was a great man, and a good patient. He didn't complain, even if he was kept waiting on a gurney for an hour in a hospital corridor before radiation treatment. He rarely got upset about his disease, save for a few nights that were too sad and private to write about, ever. Between diagnosis and death, I couldn't recall an instance when Glenn got mad or raged at fate, God, or bad luck. By nature, he wasn't an angry person.

By nature, I *was* an angry person. I'd been angry for thirty years. With increasing frequency, my poker face was cracking. I screamed "Douchebag!" out of the car window at drivers who cut me off. I hyperventilated on the phone with tech support, and had to hang up and run a mile to calm down. Judy Black style, I yelled at Maggie for leaving a major homework assignment till the last minute, and actually heard myself say, "Why do you do this to me?" Once, my friend Nancy checked her BlackBerry a few times while we were out to dinner. I said, "That's rude, selfish, and annoying. How about this, next time we go out, I'll bring a book and sit here reading while you talk about your problems." It was a snide overreaction that left us both stunned. We didn't talk for a month afterward.

Having seen so many episodes of *House,* I knew that emotional symptoms are often important diagnostic clues. My hysteria of late might have had something to do with my bumpy womb, or *hyster* in the Latin. My bilious state of mind could be related to the clogged intestine. But the bumps had been removed. The hate, however, remained.

The pathology reports were mixed.

Uterine polyps: Benign.

Rectal polyp: Abnormal cells found. The official diagnosis was carcinoma in situ, or Stage 0 cancer. The malignant cells were lazily lounging around, biding their time before rampaging throughout my innards. If I'd waited a year to have the colonoscopy, my Stage 0 mass would have gone rogue.

The GI doctor's face was more solemn than grim when he delivered the news in his office. "We also found microsatellite instability makers," he said. "It's likely your family does has Lynch syndrome." He described what I could look forward to, should the genetic mutation be confirmed, pending additional tests. I'd undergo annual screenings of my bowel as well as semiannual probes of my stomach and urinary tract. Maggie and Lucy, who had a fifty-fifty chance of inheriting the mutation from me, should start getting colonoscopies at thirty. A nonsmoker, Glenn had been told his lung cancer was a "fluke." That didn't fill me with comfort, considering the girls' chances on either side of their genetic draw.

"The risk of uterine cancer for women with Lynch syndrome is sixty percent. The ovarian cancer risk is four times that of the general population," Dr. Guts warned gently. "Screening tests for those body parts are unreliable. And since they're particularly bad cancers to get, most experts recommend prophylactic hysterectomies for Lynch syndrome women at forty."

My female bits were four years past their expiration date.

Not that I planned on using my uterus again, but I wanted to hang on to it just the same. As for the ovaries, which I was greedily milking for hormones, I was loath to part with them.

"Surgical menopause," I said. "I'll grow old overnight."

"Hysterectomies are controversial," he said. "Some women decide not to have the surgery." To help me make an informed decision, Dr. Guts gave me the contact information for a famous geneticist at the renowned Major Cancer Center in Manhattan. "He's done a lot of research on Lynch syndrome and can guide you better than I can," he said.

I felt handed off. "I'll call him."

"In the meantime," he said, "eat lots of fruits, vegetables, lean protein, and whole grains. Exercise at least three times per week for thirty minutes." It was advice that, in my lifetime of dieting, I had *never heard before.*

I must have looked upset. "How are you feeling about all this?" he asked.

"I feel . . . angry," I said.

"Understandable," he replied.

"I'm finding it hard not to hate *everyone*," I said, opening up. "My friends annoy me. My kids drive me crazy. My husband snores, really loud. He disappears to the bar for hours and comes home late for dinner. I'm a writer, and when . . ."

"A writer, really? Anything I'd know?" he asked, suddenly brightening, which I found irritating as hell.

"Do you read women's magazines?" I asked. "Like to stay current on secret sex positions and miracle pore minimizers?"

"Um, no," he said.

"*As I was saying,* when I'm expecting a check from a magazine and it's late, I want to punch in the mailbox. When I email my editor about it and she doesn't reply, I want to throw my computer out the window."

"I see."

"I even hate my cats. They clawed my lilac to death. I raised it from a tiny shoot. I really loved that bush," I said wistfully.

He nodded, made a note in his chart, and said, "I'd also strongly urge you to find a way to reduce stress."

Doctor's orders: The hate in me just had to come out.

Two

....

Why I Have No Friends, Part I

If I had to cite the main reason I became such a rabid teenage hater, it would be the lack of true friends. If I'd had one or two trustworthy pals to vent to, I might have learned to get the anger *out* instead of pouring buckets of poison ink into my journal. Even there, I didn't often write about my feelings. They were just too unwieldy, too awful to acknowledge in words. Instead, I made up slasher stories—my earliest stabs at fiction.

In the real world, where I wasn't all-powerful and all-knowing, I struggled mightily to make friends. In the middle of seventh grade, I fell in with Kerri, another chubby girl. The cabal of teasing boys' moniker for her was "whale," which, by my teenage logic, was more insulting than "cow" or "pig." After all, everyone knew a whale was fatter than a cow. Kerri had the good luck of not being in many of the tormentors' classes. Me? I was in all of them. I would gladly have traded her three daily "whales" for my fifty "pigs" in a heartbeat.

Kerri was from Millburn. Compared to Newark or Jersey City, the worst street in Millburn was as mean as a marshmallow. But middle-class Millburn was considered wealthy Short Hills's poor relation. Having been dumped by the princesses of Short Hills, though, I didn't equate address with character. I liked Kerri's tidy home within walking distance from school and her lava-lamp-lit room.

My mom distrusted Kerri on sight. No wonder. Kerri was hefty, too. Mom thought she would be a negative influence on me. When I accused Mom of being a "snob," she backed down. I started hanging at Kerri's house every afternoon. The reason we bonded at first was obvious: the enemy of my enemies is my friend. But then we found another reason to spend so much time together.

I smoked pot for the first time with Kerri. Her parents both worked and were never around. She had an older sister who would give us roaches from the ashtray of her Datsun two-door. Fingers pinched and hot, I inhaled greedily, and discovered, at thirteen, that pot was exactly what I needed, had been searching for my whole life, and could not do without.

The idea of smoking pot was just as thrilling as the result. It was illegal, and therefore naughty. My parents would have freaked out if they'd known. By day, I was a fat loser. But after school I was a super cool stoner, listening to Pink Floyd, blissed out on a beanbag chair, the curtains drawn to block out the sun. The high itself? Loved it! It was the perfect antidote to my anxieties, the rants of Judy Black, the embarrassment of "beast." I *needed* to be numb.

While I expanded my mind with pot, my brain was expanding in size. Not just *my* brain, but any teenager's brain. Thanks to the flash flood of hormones, the prefrontal cortex—the center for logic, decision making, impulse control, emotions—ballooned rapidly, tripling in size. The sudden intensity of emotion can be overwhelming for adolescents, which explains teenage recklessness, poor decision making, and stupidity. It takes ten years for teenagers to grow into their emotions. When a twenty-five-year-old gets sad, she is, sigh, *sad*. But when a fourteen-year-old gets sad, she is SAD!!!

During my friendship with Kerri, I smoked a lot of weed. And it did make me less ANGRY!!!

One afternoon Kerri's sister announced that the freeloading was over. If we wanted pot, we'd have to pay. A reasonable demand. I liked the concept of ownership, of being in control of my very own plastic baggie, hiding the stash in my room right under my parents' noses.

I stole a bill from my dad's wallet and passed a note to Kerri during study hall. "I have cash!" I wrote. "How much pot can I get for $5?"

She wrote back, "Five joints. I'll tell my sister after school."

Feeling HAPPY!!!, I put the folded piece of paper in my back jeans pocket. If all went according to plan, I would soon be in possession of five joints to call my own. (Yes, people, incredible as it might seem, once upon a time, you could buy five fat joints for five dollars.)

A couple of days later—still waiting to purchase my bag—the school principal walked into my math class. "Valerie Frankel?" he asked the room.

"Yes?" I replied.

"Please come with me."

Heart thumping, I followed him to his office, where my

mother was waiting. From the twitch of her mouth and the flash of her eyes, I knew she was in Judy Black mode, but was harnessing it in public. As soon as we got alone, she'd release the Kracken.

She said, "Let's go." We left the office. A bell rang and kids streamed out of classrooms, watching me follow my mom through the halls. I felt even more self-conscious than usual, and nervous.

In the parking lot, I asked, "What's going on?"

"Just get in the car," she said, unlocking the doors.

"Is someone hurt?"

"Get in the fucking car!" Okay, maybe it *was* better when she seethed silently.

I got in the fucking car—a Ford Bronco, black with orange racing stripes. Mom didn't speak again until we arrived home, which left me SCARED!!! and CONFUSED!!! Something major was happening. It wasn't good. I hadn't a clue what it was.

We walked into the house. Dad was waiting (not sick or dead) in the den. It was weird, seeing him at home in the middle of the day. Someone *else* had died? My sister? My brother? I was told to sit down on the couch. Mom pulled a pulpy, folded piece of paper from her shirt pocket, the blue ink runny. She held it up by the corner and said, "I found this in the dryer."

During the hanging silence of the next two seconds, the waves of revelations crashed over me. No one was sick or dead. But Mom had the note. It had fallen out of my jeans in the wash. I'd forgotten to destroy the evidence. She, they, had read it. They knew I'd been trying to buy pot. They knew who my source was. They'd probably figured out that I'd stolen money from Dad, too.

I said, "It's just pot." If I'd thought hard for a million years, I could not have come up with a lamer defense.

My mom said, "You're on drugs!"

I said, "I've never smoked before, I swear."

"You're buying it!"

"Just a little, a nickel bag," I said.

"A *what?*" Mom shrieked. "She knows the lingo! She's an addict!"

To this day, "she knows the lingo," spoken with mock-shrill hysteria, is a Frankel family catch phrase.

"It's no big deal," I insisted, seeing Mom's increasing derangement. *God,* I thought, *I wish I were stoned. Even more, I wish Mom were stoned.*

The year was 1978, the fulcrum of the swinging seventies. The entire world was getting high—including, I learned later, many of my parents' friends. I expected Mom to be totally uncool. But Dad? He had sideburns. As usual, Howie tried to calm Mom down. He was angrier at the fact that I'd stolen money than at what I'd planned to do with it. I'd shattered the trust, they accused. I was grounded for life.

Mom had made an appointment for me with a child psychologist immediately after finding the note (which, incidentally, she kept in her night-table drawer for *years*; I discovered it there when I was home from college, while looking for a manicure scissor). I went to therapy grudgingly, the next day. By then, I was over the shock of the discovery and had moved into angst-fueled resentment, hostility, and humiliation. My parents had violated *my* privacy. That note was personal! Not addressed to either of them. They might as well have read my journal! (Maybe they *had* found and read my journal—shudder.) If they were upset about the note, well, it was their fault for reading it. In fact, it was their fault I smoked pot! And now I had to have my head examined by some quack who could never *begin* to understand me, my problems, or the pain I suffered. He was a stooge for my parents, and probably a perv.

The shrink, it turned out, was nice, Jewish, mid-fifties. He seemed ancient to me at the time, bald in horn-rimmed glasses. He smiled pleasantly and showed me Rorschach ink-blots. "A mother wolf eating her young," I said of one. "A spider devouring her egg sack" of another. He gave me an IQ test. And then it was over.

Apparently, he told my parents that I had a lot of hostility toward my mother. My IQ was high, which was a shocker. Compared to my studious sister and genius brother, I'd long been considered the dunce of the family. A slow learner in elementary school, I could barely read until the third grade. My grades were average. My parents had all but written me off academically. I performed to meet their low expectations. When the shrink presented contradictory evidence, though, my parents decided that I would have to bring my grades way up. A new pressure fell on me like a ton of textbooks.

As for the matter of my ANGER!!!, the shrink told my parents that I should smoke marijuana, several times a day, until further notice.

I wished. The therapist recommended (surprise) weekly therapy sessions with him, at fifty dollars a pop (a lot back then), to talk about my feelings. Probably would have done me a world of good. But Mom and Dad gave therapy a pass. I was emotionally sound, they believed, but had fallen under the influence of that rotten Kerri kid.

"You don't need therapy," Mom declared. "You need better friends."

A month later, when my grounding ended, I lied to Mom and said I would be spending the afternoon with the straight-A-student doctor's daughter, whom she hoped would be my new best friend. Instead, I went to Kerri's. We celebrated our reunion by smoking her meager stash until it was gone. Then Kerri's sister had us pile into the Datsun to drive to her pal's house for more. Two blocks later, she drove into a tree. I remember the impact, my face hitting the driver's seat in front of me, my head snapping back and slamming into the bench headrest behind me. The sudden stillness and silence. Then Kerri's sister crying hysterically, not because she was hurt but because she knew she'd fucked up royally.

My knees buckled when I got out of the car. I fell on the street, the gravel tearing a hole in my jeans. The police arrived, sirens screaming. Everyone was okay, just rattled. I gave the cop my name and phone number. Mom picked me up ten minutes later. She didn't have to say anything—but she did, of course.

"That is *it*," she said. "You are forbidden from seeing that girl and her drug-peddling sister ever again."

I had to agree with Mom this time. Maybe it was best if I stopped hanging out with Kerri.

I walked away from the accident and our friendship without a backward glance. That unsentimental detachment—"I hate long goodbyes" in the extreme—was the first of many instances to come of my coldly severing friendships that had run their course. I left a troubled kid bleeding on the side of the road.

It was hard not to hate myself for my heartlessness. Granted, the friendship with Kerri had been flimsy. I'd used her—for companionship, to irritate Mom, for pot. She'd used me—for some of the same reasons. Except for our common enemies, there was little between us but smoke.

I n eighth grade, I hooked up with Leslie. She was also Jewish, also from Millburn. Leslie had the body of every teenage girl's dreams. Leggy, slim waisted, with high perky boobs. She wore the tightest Jordache jeans, the tiniest off-the-shoulder tops, the skinniest belts. I was in awe of her figure. She was in awe of her figure. We spent many afternoons in her bedroom admiring it as she dressed and undressed in dozens of outfits. Leslie looked great in everything. She'd pull clothes out of her closet and come up with an ensemble of a hot pink tube top with denim overalls.

"Too baggy?" she'd ask, yanking the bib like a farmer.

"You look amazing," I'd say. "I wish I were as thin as you."

Next up, a halter and pleated trousers with rainbow suspenders.

"Too disco?" she'd ask. "Too Mork?"

"I love it," I'd reply. "It makes your boobs look big."

"One more," she'd say, which meant at least three outfits to come. She put on a cowboy shirt with sparkle strands and opalescent snaps, parachute pants, and a tiny belt. I said, "It's gorgeous. Your waist is tiny."

She would put her hair up in a high pony, and we'd discuss. Then she'd put it in a low pony for a comparative analysis. I'd watch her apply makeup: dramatic navy shadow for weekend keg parties, black kohl for a daytime raccoon look, red lips, baby pink lips, mineral-bronzed cheeks. She mixed and matched makeup and outfits for hours. She was her own Barbie doll.

The object of Leslie's intense grooming was Mark, a boy who'd been the architect of my destruction by deeming me "too fat" a million years ago (actually, two), instigating the "Val is a cow" movement among his friends. Leslie spent hours plotting to "get" him. In my own small way, I helped by voting on her outfits and role-playing "if he says *this*, I'll say *this*" fantasy conversations. Back then, I failed to see the irony in facilitating the sexual satisfaction of the boy who'd judged me unworthy. In hindsight, it seemed pathologically self-negating.

Leslie was a stalker. Her attraction to Mark went beyond the bounds of teenage crush. She was on a mission, and sent by her own mother, who saw big things for her daughter. My mom dreamed that one day I would lose ten pounds. Leslie's mom dreamed that one day her daughter would marry rich. Mark was the prince of Short Hills. He wasn't particularly intelligent or interesting, but he was cute, and his family was loaded.

What else was in it for me, besides escape from home and self-negation? Leslie supplied me with another drug: sugar. Ring Dings. Pop-Tarts. Twinkies. The food my mother would have slapped out of my mouth was kept in abundant supply at Leslie's house. On the way up to her room for the daily fashion show, we'd walk through the kitchen. Leslie would grab an armful of snacks. I'd ooh and ahh at her costume changes with cheeks full of yellow cake and white frosting. Leslie noticed but didn't remark upon the pile of empty cellophane wrappers as it got higher and higher on the bed next to me. Why would she stop me? The deal was unspoken but clear. We fed each other's obsessions.

If I'd been Leslie, the boy-crazy skinny girl who dreamed about giving Mark a hand job, I would have taken comfort at the sight of the blob on the bed, shoveling in Ho Hos. She knew I would never be thin or confident enough to prance around the room in my bra and panties, squirming into Sasson jeans. Perhaps Leslie befriended me *because* I wasn't a threat. Of all the girls in school, I was the one least likely to compete with her for Mark.

Leslie's flinging her B cups in Mark's face eventually worked. He let her touch his penis. And that was the end of our friendship. She didn't need me to watch her get dressed. She had Mark to watch her get undressed.

Their relationship lasted an eternity by junior high standards: three months. When they had a fight, Leslie would call me and cry. I'd listen, give excellent advice—what I'd picked up reading teen romance novels and Judy Blume. When they made up, she'd disappear again.

I missed her abstractly. Since she'd cut me off, I had to spend my afternoons at home again. My junk food intake dropped dramatically. On a prurient level, I enjoyed being exposed to her near-nudity. I loved the mountain of junk food she offered like a bribe or payment. She basked in my envy and compliments. I bathed in the soft comfort of sugar and saturated fat. We were like two toddlers in the same room, content to pursue our own interests, and not really interacting with each other.

Eventually, Mark broke up with Leslie for good. But she never called me again. By her lights, her months of sexual experience earned her a spot at the popular girls' table. She pursued them with characteristic determination. The cool girls were harder to seduce than Mark, though. I watched her futile attempts from afar, snidely enjoying the show.

In my next attempt at friendship, I resolved to find someone with whom I had a common interest. That brought me to Nina, yet another chubby Jewish girl, this one from Short Hills, who was also a chronic dieter. Her mother was an anorexic who encouraged Nina's rice-cake eating, but in a nice way, a supportive way. I wonder if her mom's soft-sell attempt to get her to lose weight was as damaging to Nina's psyche as my mom's relentless criticism was to mine. I'd go to Nina's house after school and we'd plan diets and meals on graph paper with colored markers. We kept a list of foods and their calorie counts.

"Celery is negative calories," said Nina's mom, smoking and reading our charts on the kitchen table over our shoulders. "If you did nothing but eat celery all day long, you'd lose weight. Iceberg lettuce, too."

With bags of celery, Nina and I sat down in front of the TV and started chewing. Two hours later, three pounds of celery gone, Nina asked, "Think it's working?"

"Maybe," I said. "Definitely *not* hungry."

"I feel thinner," said Nina, placing a palm on her bloated belly, which was crammed with fiber.

I had the most beautiful poop of my life the next day, and

the day after. And the day after. Nina and I conducted similar eating experiments with rice cakes, and leaves of spinach. We talked about boys in a fanciful way, neither of us hoping or believing that any of them would go out with us. I remember laughing constantly with Nina, her crooked smile with a cute chipped tooth (from eating all that celery?), making up dirty jokes about giant erections.

I thought this friendship would last. When we parted ways at the end of ninth grade for the summer break, I fully expected to be her best friend when school started again. But in September she surprised everyone by showing up to tenth grade skinny. She'd lost twenty pounds at camp. I was happy for her but felt abandoned—and JEALOUS!!!, of course. She was drawn into another crowd, and I had another lonely year of false starts.

My last attempt at teenage female bonding was in eleventh grade. I became part of a threesome with Olive and Penny. Compared to my previous friends, Olive and Penny were exotic creatures. A Catholic and a Mormon, they came from huge families. Olive had four brothers and sisters. Penny had seven siblings.

Although their parents didn't nag them about grades or their weight, the two had problems aplenty. Olive's parents were loving, but they struggled financially and worked odd hours—her dad was a bartender—to make ends meet. Penny's parents were hyper-religious, with strictly enforced rules. I remember Penny's puffy red face when we went by her house after school one day. She'd been grounded, so we sat on her front lawn. I asked her if she'd been crying.

She said, "My father just punished me for lying about where I was yesterday afternoon." She'd been with her greasy boyfriend. Olive and I were baffled by Penny's attraction to him, except that he infuriated her parents.

Incredibly, Penny laughed. "It was worth it," she said.

Like I said, weird. Curious. Exotic.

Often, Olive, Penny, and I went into New York City by train, picked up boys in Washington Square, and made out with them on benches. We bought dime bags of pot from dealers, and then smoked with them in plain view. The flouting of convention and risk to personal safety terrified and entranced me. We'd bring a couple of six-packs of Meisterbrau to the town park after dark. Olive would take tiny sips, one after the other, delicate and feminine. It seemed as if she were barely drinking at all, but the pyramid of empties next to her on the basketball blacktop grew higher and higher. Unlike Penny, who chugged until she puked in the bushes and then chugged some more, Olive lent a methodical purposefulness to her drinking.

"Are you drunk?" I asked her. It was hard to tell. She'd had five beers, which was four over my limit. She seemed okay, but she was spacey when sober, too.

She turned toward me, her eyes swimming, barely able to focus, and slurred, "I'm fine." She blinked, swayed, and opened another can. It was scary, and sad, her quiet quest for oblivion.

I appointed myself Olive's protector. I'd watch over her, make sure no harm came to her, even as she stumbled through city streets, blind drunk, going up to strangers and laughing in their faces.

When I turned seventeen, I got my driver's license and the

use of a hunter green Volkswagen Sirocco. I was our getaway driver. I used my weekend waitress earnings to buy beer, cigarettes, and gas.

Sometimes I felt used. I kept these misgivings to myself. It wasn't Olive and Penny's fault they didn't have cars. We were a collective, gladly sharing our resources. We would drive all over town, looking for something to do, blowing streams of blue pot smoke out the cracked car windows. We drove to clubs in Manhattan, using fake IDs to get into punk rock shows on the Lower East Side. We sneaked into movies. Loitered at the mall. Sat in the park on the swings and crushed beer cans with rocks.

Although we were a tight trio, we had peripheral friends. One was a boy, Paul, who was madly—he thought secretly—in love with Olive. We weren't that close, but he called me one day when I was at home watching *General Hospital,* and none too pleased to be interrupted. He danced around the point for a few minutes before hitting me over the head with it.

"I heard Olive and Penny talking about you today," he said.

Preemptive gulp. I had fifth-wheel fears sporadically. The idea of the two of them talking about me behind my back made my stomach churn. "What did they say?"

"I'm only telling you because I think you should know," he said. "They called you 'the chauffeur.' They laughed that you were their driver and piggy bank. And also that you were a fat Jew."

Since Paul was a fat Jew himself, I understood why he'd felt the urge to drop that bomb on me. The phrase "piggy bank" hurt. "Piggy" was only too reminiscent of my torment in junior high. I'd thought all that was behind me. But as Paul faithfully—and, as it turned out, truthfully—reported, my friends as well as my enemies hated me for being over-weight.

I hung up, watched the cliffhanger end of *GH,* and cried for a while. I felt hollowed out, alone, back to the place I'd always expected to return. Not SAD!!! really. Worn down. Humili-ated. I could hear Olive and Penny laughing about me, the mean way they laughed at other people.

Recently, a friend told me about going on a church over-night trip in high school. The other kids slept in a motel while she slept on the bus in the parking lot because the girls were so vicious to her. One good outcome: She got through the night reading *Rich Man, Poor Man,* and discovered the joy of escaping into books (she is now a novelist). Another pal still shudders with shame at her own participation when a group of girls cor-nered a target and chanted "fat" until she cried.

Child development experts call this type of behavior "rela-tional aggression," or intentionally destroying another person's standing in a group through nonviolent emotional manipulation. The usual culprits are teenage girls. To inflict damage, adolescent boys use their fists. Girls use their mouths. Gossiping, back-stabbing, betraying confidences, lying, excluding, humiliating—these are the weapons in the relational aggressor's arsenal. Why do girls do it? For fun, sport, entertainment, a cure for boredom, and to test the boundaries of their capacity for cruelty, and their target's willingness to take it.

I'd reached my limit for adolescent cruelty years before. One cutting comment—although, technically, "chauffeur,"

"piggy bank," and "fat Jew" were three separate comments—
was enough for me to exit any relationship.

Olive called me later that evening, as usual. "Come pick
me up," she said.

I said, "I'm busy," and hung up.

Penny called next, and asked, "What're you doing?"

They'd talked to each other, clearly. I said, "Just busy." I
went in my room and cranked the Ramones to hide my crying from my family.

After a couple of days of being "busy," Penny and Olive
realized something was wrong. Under pressure during lunch
period in the cafeteria, I told them what Paul had told me.
They didn't deny it.

Olive said, "We were kidding."

Penny said, "We just said it to freak him out."

Olive said, "You should have seen the look on his face!"

"You would have laughed, too," Penny said. "It's annoying, your being so sensitive. Can't you take a joke?"

I was more wounded by their "apology" than I'd been by
their betrayal.

I told Olive's sister, Violet, what had happened. Violet was
a grade older, someone I looked up to and thought of as a
friend. (Violet is still my close friend, the only one I kept from
high school.) She was horrified by what Olive had said about
me. On my behalf, she stepped in and set her sister straight,
telling her she'd been thoughtless and mean, and had mis-
treated a good friend.

Olive seemed genuinely contrite after Violet reamed her
out. Driven by fatigue and loneliness, I started hanging with

Olive and Penny again, but it was never the same. The essential trust was gone. Every time I drove them anywhere, I felt uncomfortable, and they were uneasy passengers. Penny started spending more time with her greasy boyfriend, and eventually drifted away. Olive and I were absorbed into a larger clique of freaks and punks who DJ'd for the school radio station. The DJ booth became my regular hangout. I felt more secure as part of group than I had in a one-on-one or one-on-two situation.

Female friendships: Don't believe the nurturing, supportive hype. *Sex and the City*? Try *Vex and the Shitty*. Maybe it was my fault. I had a knack for picking pals who brought out the worst in me, and vice versa. We encouraged each other's bad behavior and destructive obsessions. Our emotional bonds proved to be flimsy, unreal. Either born a skeptic or hammered into one, I found that my suspicions—Did she *really* give a shit? Did I? Was she a user? Was I?—always turned out to be correct.

In high school and college I spied girls who made friendship look easy. They'd walk down the street, through the halls, around campus, their arms slung across each other's shoulders, laughing at some private joke. As an easy defense, I decided to feel smugly superior to them. I was too complicated to have such silly relationships. If they noticed me at all, those happy girls probably felt sorry for me, or were repelled.

It wasn't only that I wouldn't join any club that would have me as a member.

No club would have me as a member!

By nineteen, I'd had enough of girls. With rare exception, all of my college friends were guys. Friendships with men were easier, more fun—until I slept with them, of course.

Three

. . . .

Yes, *Really*

Brooklyn Heights in springtime. You can smell the splendor. It's a crime against nature to be a hater in June, especially on my block, the most charming in the neighborhood (seriously, there've been polls). Cherry and apple trees line the sidewalks. My neighbors take competitive pride in their flower boxes and stoop planters. The Victorian brownstones are lovingly maintained. A landmarked district— every building has to be preserved according to its historical period—Brooklyn Heights was built as a bedroom community for the barons of Wall Street in the mid-nineteenth century. The brownstone we live in dates back to 1861, and probably looked much the same then as it does now.

Except, in 1861 the streets weren't paved, cars didn't exist, and parking wasn't a blood sport. For years, I parked my Volvo wagon on the street, circling for hours to find a spot, moving it a few times a week as per the city's alternate-side-of-the-street-parking laws. While racing home early from work to get in my car, zip it across the street, and then sit there for an hour until 6:00 PM, when that side became legal, I realized it was not cost-efficient to spend so much time parking. I could spend that time writing a magazine article or three to pay for a permanent spot in the garage a few blocks away, which was what I did.

Even though the garage spot costs almost as much as my health insurance (I wish I were joking), I consider it money well spent. The car is safe from sideswiping, theft, snow, vandalism, and tickets. I am relieved of aggravation. But there've been times when I was forced to park in front of my building anyway. When I load the girls' camp trunks into the car. Or after my annual geranium binge at the local nursery for my container garden.

On one particular day, I had a full trunk of groceries from Fairway to unload. A few blocks from home, I started visualizing a big juicy spot, wide open, right in front of my brownstone. But this power of wishful thinking was no match for parking in Brooklyn Heights. Sure enough, when I arrived I found my block tightly packed with vehicles. I'd have to double-park and risk getting a ticket. Twice I'd done this—left my trunk open, hazards on, signaling to the overzealous parking police that I'd be right back—only to return five minutes later to find a ticket on the windshield.

So that day, I was resigned to racing up and down three flights of stairs with the groceries, the whole time fretting a summons. Then I noticed a BMW, motor running, taillights on, parked a few doors down from my building.

I pulled up alongside to ask if the driver was pulling out or pulling in. I couldn't get her attention at first. She was on the phone. I waited for her to notice my car idling next to her. Nothing. I leaned through my open window and gently rapped on hers.

She looked up, annoyed to be interrupted.

No, I thought, and my throat went dry. *Not her.*

Nearly all the residents of my block are neighborly. Even if we haven't been introduced, or lack social and professional intersection, we'd acknowledge one another anyway. A smile. A nod. Common freaking courtesy. But a few of my neighbors are above plebian politeness. I think of this coven of middle-aged white women as the Bitches.

The BMW driver on her phone? The Biggest Bitch of All.

The BBoA and I *had* been introduced, by my then-downstairs neighbors, a convivial empty-nester couple. I was sitting with them on our stoop one day, enjoying a sunny afternoon when the BBoA strolled by. I'd seen her before, and knew she lived on the block, had a couple of kids. The empty-nesters greeted the BBoA and invited her to take a load off and join us on the stoop. She accepted the offer. The four of us had a pleasant if insubstantial conversation for fifteen minutes before the BBoA got up, said goodbye, and continued on her way. A nice little urban moment, the kind that warmed the heart, made me feel grounded in my home, block, and city.

The very next day, Maggie, Lucy, and I were walking to the deli on the corner when I saw the BBoA heading toward us from the opposite direction. We passed each other. I smiled and said, "Hi there!" She? Completely ignored me. It was as if

(1) we hadn't talked on my stoop a mere twelve hours ago, (2) I was made of thin air, and (3) she had the *Memento* disease and forgot everything immediately after she'd lived it.

Lucy said, "Awkward."

Maggie asked, "Does anyone feel a sudden chill?"

I decided to cut the BBoA some slack. Maybe she was distracted. Even though she was six inches away, perhaps she hadn't seen me. Maybe she was partially blind—and deaf. She might be on drugs. Or drunk off her ass at ten o'clock in the morning. Or got fired. Or caught her husband masturbating to Internet porn. Or caught her son masturbating to Internet porn. Or maybe she was ignoring me because I was unworthy of acknowledgment. Maybe, just maybe, this woman was a snob of inconceivable heinousness.

I gave her the benefit of the doubt and went with "she was distracted and/or hadn't seen me." But I crossed paths with her on the block a few times a week. Same thing, over and over again, the blank stare at a spot three inches in front of her nose when she blew by. One day I was standing on the corner, talking to another neighbor, when the BBoA approached and stopped to say hello—to the person I was speaking to, not me. We were reintroduced. She acted as if she'd never laid eyes on me before.

Our third official introduction was at a holiday party at the empty-nesters' apartment.

He re-reintroduced us, saying, "You two have already met."

She said, "I don't *think* so."

Was I ugly? Did I smell? Was I too nice for her? Too Jewish? In my book, if someone had no memory of three separate face-to-face formal introductions, that person was a self-important ass, brain damaged, or both. To forget someone's *name* was forgivable. I got Kate, Karen, and Carrie confused. I've said, "Forgive me, what was your name again?" many times. Since I remembered context, who'd introduced us, when and where, forgetting a name wasn't too offensive (I hoped). But forgetting someone's *face*, after being introduced *three times,* and seeing each other a few times a week? Even if you were perpetually stoned or on crack? I didn't see how that was possible.

Some unfortunates are blighted with a cognitive impairment called prosopagnosia, or "face blindness." They simply cannot place faces. Usually prosopagnosiacs also fail to recognize locations, cars, facial expressions. It is a horrible condition. Imagine forgetting your kids' smiles? Some sufferers can't identify their own faces in a photo array. But I've witnessed the BBoA recognize people she knows. Prosopagnosia is not her excuse.

Her snubbing seemed hostile, intentional—yes, just like the girls in junior high who dumped and shunned me. At least Amy and Brenda had ignored me for a reason. Their social standing was at stake. The BBoA? Maybe she feared that if she opened her mouth to say good morning, I'd snatch out her tongue.

Our schedules fell into sync. When I walked Lucy to school in the morning, we'd pass the BBoA with her dog. Not once, all year long, did she look at us. Not even a sidelong glance, a peek out of the corner of her eye, a detection of movement. Nine people out of ten acknowledge that another human being is within their breathing space. Chimps in the jungle bare teeth when another is in close range. This woman didn't have the instincts of a feces-flinging ape.

The other two Bitches? One was a petite blonde with long straight hair. Like the BBoA, the blonde had a set of magic blinders that made other people on the street completely invisible. She had a regal posture, a ballerina's gait: shoulders back, chin up, spine elongated. The combination of her ramrod straightness and dark eyes (black eyes, a doll's eyes) gave her an eerie, tortured aura. When I learned she was a professor of nineteenth-century Russian literature, I wasn't surprised. Unlike the BBoA, the ballerina would watch you coming. She'd scrutinize you as you walked toward her, the doll's eyes moving up and down your body, and then, when you were five feet away, when a polite smile, a nod, a "morning" was called for, she'd go blank, as if in a trance, almost as if she'd been hit on the head.

Over sangria with my old friend Violet, I described the ballerina's strange process, the long examination, and then the last-minute look-away.

"That's called 'pulling a Williamsburg,'" Violet said.

"This is a thing?" I asked.

"It is in Williamsburg," she said.

Williamsburg is the neo-hipster Brooklyn nabe where Violet lived for fifteen years, way before the first juice bar, hoodie boutique, beer garden, or bowling alley opened.

"It's a classic move," she said. "The key is to glance away at the very last second. Checking your iPod or reading a subway

poster. It means you're too cool to lower yourself to acknowledge someone of lesser coolness—even if you know her. Have
I mentioned lately that I'm the oldest person on my entire
block?"

The insecurity of youth might explain Williamsburgian
aloofness. But the BBoA was ten years *older* than me. The ballerina was around my age, but she looked older. Museum-
quality hauteur was prematurely aging.

The ballerina and I did have one thing in common. She
was an author. I was shocked to see her photo on one of the
publishing blogs I read every day. She'd written a memoir
about her struggle with chronic pain. Apparently, she'd been
in an accident twenty years ago and sustained a lower back
injury that she thought (wrongly) had healed. Two years ago,
out of the blue, her back started hurting. Doctors discovered
the old, unhealed injury. If it'd been properly treated way
back when, she'd have been fine. Unfortunately, it hadn't
and she wasn't. She'd reached the tipping point of decades of
cumulative nerve damage and lived in medically managed
agony.

I read an excerpt of her book and instantly felt like a jerk for
labeling her a Bitch. "She's in constant pain," I said to my husband, Steve. "No wonder she seems so cold."

"How long have we lived on the block?"

"Five years," I said.

"When did her pain start?"

"Two years ago."

"Was she friendly before then?"

No. Not in the slightest. You could sympathize with

someone with a chronic physical condition, I decided, and still think she was a bitch.

The last Bitch, a tall willowy boho type who made jewelry she sold to other housewives at parties, was actually okay. She smiled and nodded when I passed her on the block. I'd seen her as far away as Smith Street—two neighborhoods over—and had received perfunctory attention. She gave me flyers for her jewelry sales. At the very least, she was neighborly enough to take my money. Boho wasn't actually a bitch. I just grouped her in with the others because I'd heard from Tracy, a daffy, warm woman who'd lived in Brooklyn Heights her whole life, that these three women took turns hosting a regular brunch, and that they occasionally opened it up to other women from the block.

"Have you been invited yet?" Tracy asked me.

By the Bitches? I was *invisible* to two out of three of them. How could they even have found me to invite me? I wouldn't have gone anyway, even if they'd begged me/paid me/gone down on me/washed my car/cleaned my oven/weeded my garden. I loved Tracy for her faith in my brunch desirability, but I wasn't on the Bitches' radar.

I described the BBoA's behavior to my friend Lynn, who happened to be a psychologist. "Why do you care if this woman says hello to you?" she said. "You don't even know her name."

"I'm merely curious about her psychological motivation," I stated falsely.

"Why *would* someone pretend another person didn't exist?" Lynn asked. "You're right, it could be snobbery. Selective blindness; she only sees what she wants to see. She might be a hostile person who gets a kick out of being rude. All of that or none of it might be true. But it doesn't matter why she does what she does. What matters is how it makes you feel."

"I find it hard not to hate her," I said. "No one wants to feel invisible."

"So make yourself visible," said Lynn. "Next time you see her, scream, 'Howdy, neighbor!' I'd have fun with it. Deflate her power that way."

"Or just resolve to be a strong confident woman who doesn't seek the approval or acknowledgment of others to feel good about herself," I said.

"I thought you'd resolved to express your anger or stop pretending it didn't exist," she said. "Don't cop out."

So, there I was, car trunk full of groceries, parked alongside the BBoA, doing the hand gestures known to city drivers around the world to signify "Are you leaving that spot anytime this century?"

BBoA continued talking on her cell. She glanced at me through the car window—registering my physical presence— and vaguely nodded that she was going to drive away.

Fine. Great. I backed up to give her plenty of room and waited for her to pull out.

And waited. A minute went by. Then two. She was still blabbing away, her motor running, taillights on, but not putting her car in gear and vacating the space, even though she knew I was waiting for it.

If our positions had been reversed, I would immediately have pulled out and then parked on the illegal side of the street to finish my conversation. I would have felt anxious about making someone wait for . . . five minutes now, ice cream in the trunk a puddle, surely. Even if I were negotiating the release of hostages on that cell phone, I'd still move.

Perhaps she'd forgotten about me. I could toot my horn, but that would be too much. I could pull up, do the pantomime of "moving *today,* dumb ass?" again. I could get out of my car and loiter in her view. That seemed to be the smartest idea: a gentle reminder that I was waiting. I got out, walked over to her window, leaned down, and looked inside.

She saw me, all right. Not proficient at reading lips, I was pretty sure I got the gist of what she mouthed at me: "Wait one goddamn minute," or something along those lines.

I nodded, got back in my car. For thirty seconds I contemplated the Old Way, how I would have handled this situation in "Me, 12" style. I would have resumed my vigil, ambiguous smile plastered on, rage steaming from my head, fogging the windows. I'd have wiped a hole in the windshield to watch until she finally left, put my hand out of the window to wave in phony gratitude. For the rest of the day, I'd have told and retold the story of her poor parking etiquette, dumping my anger on my friends and husband.

But not today. Today, I'd be the bitch, see how she liked it. Risking a ticket, I pulled my car parallel to hers, completely blocking her in, and proceeded to unload my packages, parading right in front of her BMW, carrying my bags up the stairs, unpacking the frozen goods, arranging the produce in the crisper drawers. Taking my sweet mofo time.

Done unpacking, I came back down to the street. BBoA was standing outside her car now, burning a hole in my front door with her malevolent stare. I felt a pang of fear, I'll admit, and decided to say, "Sorry about that!" in a perky, sunny voice like you'd hear on a dishwashing liquid commercial. But the BBoA got in the first word.

"Really?" she asked.

Not "Really?" in the sense of "Surely you jest!" No, she used the 2009 intonation. The Joaquin Phoenix on *Letterman* vernacular, what people used to mean when they said, "Seriously?" The BBoA's "Really?" was short for, "Are you *really* that petty? Is your rudeness *really* within the realm of comprehension? Do I *really* have to deal with a lowly excuse for a human being like you?"

I shrugged, got in my car, and drove away toward the garage.

Shaking a bit, my heart pounding, I did a quick emotions check. I felt . . . nervous. Excited. Giddy. A tad guilty for being so obnoxious, but I could live with that.

It was a baby step. Not as if I'd torn the Bitch a new one or taught her a lesson she wouldn't soon forget on the appropriate expression of justifiable anger. But I'd made myself visible, and taken back some power. I'd also lost some fear, specifically, the fear of being judged. Oh, the Bitch would judge me, all right. She might even come up with a nickname for me (The Freak? The Volvonator?). So what? I'd been vindictive and rude, which instantly (like magic) had relieved my stress. Dr. Guts would have applauded.

Hating *is* good for you. Gwyneth Paltrow might be on to something.

As I drove to the garage, I laughed imagining my next encounter with the BBoA. She'd walk toward me, her dog on a leash, and I'd shout, "Hey, lady! Find any good parking spots lately?!"

More likely, if she saw me coming, she'd probably cross the street to avoid me. Scratch that: She'd *definitely* see me coming. And if she should cross the street? More sidewalk for me.

Four

How to Love the Man You Hate

As the nights warm in June, a woman's thoughts turn, nostalgically, romantically, to her ex-boyfriends. Or, that was how it seemed, since every "beach novel" on display at Barnes and Noble that month asked the question "What if?" about a love from the past who got away. I circled and recircled the New Fiction table, picking up books, reading the cover flap, putting them down with a disgusted *ecch*. What was the appeal of this plot device? Beat me.

Fantasizing about a reunion with an old flame? My vagina shriveled at the thought. I'd be happy never to lay eyes on my exes again. My sentiments were "As if!" not "What if?"

I'd rather read a novel about a woman stricken with selective amnesia who forgets every wince-worthy moment of her romantic past. I wish I could. In my early dating life, I was a needy-greedy girlfriend, always wanting more reassurance, promises, commitment. I counted and recounted the number of dates, sex sessions, money spent, nights together, months as a couple. If it lasted six months, the relationship would pass the Test of Time. Chronically dissolving after three months, my relationships barely qualified to take the Quiz of Time. Boyfriends pulled back as I pushed forward. And when they dumped me, I grieved as if I'd lost a limb. Oh, the drama, sobbing into my pillow, calling friends every hour to give the feelings update. I begged men for a second (or third) chance, calling, hanging up, calling, crying, laughing at the absurdity, begging again. Groveling did win me a few stays of execution. I thought, "Shame is underrated. Pride was for single women."

I met my first major New York boyfriend, Tom, when I was a fact-checker at the short-lived, self-consciously titled *New York Woman* magazine. He was a thirty-year-old freelance copy editor. I was twenty-three and thought it was the height of sophistication to date an older man. Tom was an aspiring journalist (like me) and had been published in a few big magazines (unlike me). I was impressed with the eloquent way he talked about writing, his many editor and author friends. His breadth of random information amazed me. If there were a Trivial Pursuit or *Jeopardy!* Olympics, Tom would medal.

Before we had our first date—quasi-arranged by our mutual friend, the copy chief (henceforth CC) at *NYW*—Tom read part of the mystery novel I was writing at night and told me, "It's brilliant. Do you know how good you are?" Picture me, stars twinkling in my eyes.

The pièce de résistance—not that I was resisting—was Tom's apartment. He lived in a large one-bedroom in Greenwich Village, the charmingly old Manhattan neighborhood I longed to move to one day. At that time, I lived in a run-down floor-through apartment in Park Slope, Brooklyn, with two roommates. My bedroom, in real estate vernacular, was the "pocket room," a five-by-eight-foot rectangle with a sliding door. Big enough for a futon and not much else.

So Tom was older, wiser, more experienced (except sexually), and he had a nice place. He was nothing like the dropouts and mamma's boys I'd dated thus far. When my roommates went out of town one weekend, I invited him to Brooklyn to cook him dinner. I bought an antique lace dress at a vintage clothing store and wore it with nothing underneath. I served him thin marinara sauce on overcooked spaghetti, which he said was delicious. Afterward, I stood in the living room, shed the antique lace, and waved him in for dessert. He looked at me, eyes glowing, and said, "Is this really happening?"

By "this," I thought he meant finally finding the woman of his dreams. Then again, he might've been talking about sex with the lights on. He seemed to love whatever I did—dressed or undressed—and I gobbled up the approval. Once, in bed, he said, "You could make a man come just by looking at his dick." (FYI: I subsequently tried to give an "eye job" to other guys, but so far, no success.)

We'd been together for two months when he said, "It's kind of gross, how fast you eat." We were at a pizza parlor. I was reaching for my third slice, and he was still nibbling his first. His dream girl, apparently, ate like a sparrow, not a vulture. Thereafter, whenever we ate together, I was self-conscious about speed. That was the first time Tom had made a modification request to fit his girlfriend specs. It wasn't the last.

I arrived at his apartment after work and dropped my purse and coat on the floor. He said, "You're such a slob." Embarrassed, I rushed to pick up my stuff and hang it neatly on the door. We went to an art-house movie. He called my observations about plot and character "naive" and "sophomoric." I told him a story about how I'd hidden the toilet paper before my roommate went into the bathroom with a magazine. My other roommate and I waited for the inevitable, counted down, and, on cue, heard a scream for help. It was funny at the time. When I told Tom, he shrugged and said, "It's just another selfish Val story."

We went to dinner with some of his friends—his age, married with kids—and the conversation turned to politics. I started to weigh in, but Tom cut me off and warned me not to "embarrass yourself." His friends laughed and told me to pontificate away. But I could barely open my mouth for the rest of the endless meal—even to eat, so it had to be really bad—seeing myself through their eyes. In a weird way, I was flattered. I'd never been an older guy's piece of ass before.

The final blow came at a Bruce Springsteen concert at Long Island's Nassau Coliseum. My sister, Alison, speed-dialed Ticketmaster and, incredibly, scored four seats. She invited Tom and me to go with her and Dan, her husband. Despite growing up in New Jersey, where infants were swaddled in "Born to Run" blankets, I hadn't seen Springsteen in concert. His latest album, *Tunnel of Love,* came out around the same time Tom and I started dating. A concept album, it told the story, song by song, of a romantic relationship, from the passion and optimism of the beginning (side one) to the disillusionment and regret of the ending (side two). I played side one continually, aligning the joy in the grooves with our new love. I couldn't wait to hear it live, with Tom.

Although I'd met many of his friends, I hadn't trotted Tom

out to meet mine. I feared they'd call him an egghead. For one thing, he had an oversized cranium, like a caricature of an evil scientist. Also, he was an outspoken intellectual snob, hated anything too popular, and was always spouting obscure bits of esoterica he found fascinating but that were kind of boring to other people. Alison and Dan were closer to Tom's age, and more intellectual than I was. They might like his random fac-toids, I thought. The concert double date would be a significant step.

The evening of the concert, Tom and I took the train to Long Island. Alison and Dan picked us up at the station to drive to the arena. The four of us made easy conversation. Alison and Dan, both journalists, had a couple of mutual friends with Tom. He was smooth and smart. I beamed at the camaraderie.

Once we got inside, we were all impressed by the seats, fifth row center, close enough to catch sweat. The E-Street Band came on. The audience exploded. Alison, Dan, and I stood on our chairs, sang, screamed, cheered. Springsteen in his prime: a miracle of music and energy. A few tunes in, I looked over at Tom, expecting to, I don't know, high-five him or something. He was not in a fist-thumping mood. He seemed upset. I screamed in his ear, "What's wrong?"

He screamed back, "It's too loud!"

I yelled, "What? I can't hear you."

He shouted, "I don't like your singing. I want to leave."

My singing had been known to crack mirrors. But there was no way my voice could be heard above the wall of sound. I said, "So go," meaning he should check out the concession area, or the bathroom, get some air, whatever.

He shook his head. "I want to go *home, now.*"

Unless he was puking, swooning, or gushing blood from an open wound, I was not going to leave this concert. I said, "It'll be over soon."

Three electric hours later, it was. I loved every minute of it.

Tom, on the other hand, acted as if he'd been tortured on the rack. Picture it: thirty thousand fans on their feet, having the time of their lives, and one evil scientist in the fifth row sitting with his legs crossed, arms folded over his chest, hunched over, grimacing. A few times, I tried to rally Tom's enthusiasm. When Springsteen sang the album's titular tune, what I thought of as our theme song, I reached for his hand. He violently jerked away from me.

When the house lights came up, Tom snarled, "Can we leave *now?*" I asked if he was feeling okay. He snapped, "What do *you* care?"

Alison and Dan eyed each other suspiciously. She asked Tom if anything was wrong. He said, "I'm not talking to *you,* either."

I was mortified he'd be so rude to Alison and Dan. They'd bought the tickets, given us a ride, made him the center of attention before the show.

It was a quiet ride in Alison and Dan's car to the Long Island Railroad station. While waiting for the train to take us back to the city, I repeatedly asked Tom to explain what was wrong, why he was so angry. It came down to this: He'd wanted to leave, and I hadn't. He considered my refusal an unholy act of selfishness that he might not soon forgive. I countered that his asking me to leave had been selfish. If he'd really been miserable, he could've found a quiet place to wait. He knew how I'd been looking forward to the show, how I listened to the album obsessively. He could plainly see how much fun I was having.

If the situation had been reversed and I wasn't enjoying an event of his choosing, I would have begged his forgiveness and slipped away or soldiered through to please him. I'd already done it many times, at dinners with his friends and watching art-house films. But Tom didn't care about "another absurd hypothetical" from me. I'd failed a test I hadn't known I was taking.

On the phone the next day, Alison said she'd liked Tom "at first." She urged me to look at him objectively, to raise the veil of idealized romance I'd draped over him. Dan's verdict was more direct. "What a crybaby," he said.

Maybe so. But he was *my* crybaby.

Not for much longer, however. Soon after the concert Tom became stumped for things to say. It was a major shift. At dinner, he alternated between fitful silence and heavy sighing. He asked snippily, "So. Read any good books lately?" A first-date question. We'd been together for four months. When I told him about my day, he'd find a nugget of bad behavior to fixate on and would spend the rest of the night explaining why my actions had been wrong, stupid, immature, and selfish.

Why did I take it? My habitual poker-facing was well established by then. I was also afraid I'd make things worse if I complained. I believed, with all my heart, that I was one homemade dinner or crackerjack blowjob away from making him love me again. I wanted to go back to the early days, when he'd said, "Is this really happening?"

Another of Tom's memorable lines: "It's not you, it's me."

Believe me, it sounded fresh in 1988. He used it for the opener of a comprehensive breakup speech. I think he'd memorized it. He sat me down on his couch and said that I deserved a man who (1) was as energetic and passionate as I was, (2) was open-minded and adventurous, (3) shared my tastes and interests, (4) was more compatible than he was, (5) genuinely admired my writing, (6) didn't mind my not using deodorant, and (7) could forgive my occasionally unshaven legs. (From that day on, I used deodorant daily, applying it with religious zeal. I also became a hair-removal maven, shaving, waxing, threading, eventually spending a fortune on laser treatments.)

Tom continued, speaking with wide-eyed earnestness, that I should find a replacement who (8) thought I looked sexy in miniskirts, (9) was excited by larger-than-average nipples, (10) found anything of intellectual value in those trashy romance and mystery novels I loved so dearly, (11) had similarly lowbrow taste in film, and, yes, (12) could stand the overrated, crassly commercial musical platitudes of Bruce Springsteen.

He wrapped up his breakup speech by repeating the "it's not you" line. I could see he was proud of that, using the decisive phrase as a framing device. Even as I sat there devastated, I had to admire his effective use of repetition.

Then he stopped talking and stared at me, waiting for the waterfalls. It was my cue to cry, claw out his eyes, or run out of his apartment in hysterics.

But I felt numb, hollow. The regret, self-loathing, and lone-liness hit soon enough, and hard—but not until I got home. My only solace? This heartbreak wasn't my fault. It was *his* fault. He'd said so himself, twice. I gathered my purse, put on my jacket, yanked my miniskirt as low as I could, and left.

The great pining began. Intermittent crying, permanent puffy eyes. I played the *Tunnel of Love* side-two sob-along track "When You're Alone" five hundred times in the coming months. The poignant lyric: "Nobody knows where love goes, but when it goes, it's gone, gone."

Everyone at the office knew Tom; he was a regular free-lancer in the copy department. They'd been keeping tabs on our romance. The editors and assistants at the magazine sympathized with me. They accused Tom of using me for sex, taking advantage of my inexperience in love, luring me in, and then throwing me away. I defended him, somehow forgetting his insensitivity at the end, and remembered only the kindness of the beginning.

I asked CC, "Would you mind not hiring Tom for a little while? Just for one issue, until I feel stronger?"

She said, "I'm sorry, Val, but your hurt feelings can't be a factor in my hiring decisions. I need him for closing next week. So brace yourself."

A gentleman after the fact, Tom turned down the work.

CC's desk was on the other side of a flimsy cubicle partition wall from mine. I could overhear her end of phone conversations as clearly as if I were sitting on her lap. "Hey, Tom!" she trilled when he called. She laughed uproariously. "You are *too* funny!" Silence. "Sounds like you had an *amazing* time." And then the killer: "How old is she again?"

Although CC was, allegedly, my friend, she seemed to take sadistic pleasure in my pain. But I rationalized it, reminding myself that she and Tom were old pals. They had every right to talk. But her broadcasting that Tom was dating several women, while I sat inches away on the verge of tears, was

unjustifiably mean. This woman was a staunch vegan envi-
ronmentalist, a fierce lover and protector of plants and animals. But people? Especially young women she felt superior
to? We were fair game.

I let her fix me up *again,* with a friend of hers who was,
I learned on our one short date, a twice-my-age unemployed
alcoholic with a facial tic. He barely spoke and didn't make
eye contact. When I told CC I wasn't into him, she accused
me of being too picky, and said I'd be lucky to do better.
Eventually, I was fired from *NYW*—for a fact-checker, I had
a flexible definition of what constituted a "fact." The best part
of leaving that job was getting away from CC.

The epilogue on Tom: About six months after my first
husband, Glenn, died, a mutual acquaintance reported that
she'd run into Tom at a party. He said to her, "I heard Val is
single again," and confessed he'd often looked back on our
relationship and regretted ending it so abruptly.

He sent an email. The content was a longer version of
"Sorry about your husband. But enough about that. Here's
what I've been doing for the last fifteen years." He included
links to his business Web site. Tom never got around to writing his literary masterpiece, but he had started a company that
organized mystery weekends and highbrow scavenger hunts
in several cities nationwide. His brainy urban adventures won
raves in print and broadcast media. He'd turned his esoteric
trivial knowledge into a thriving business. "Bravo, bastard,"
I thought, reading a few reviews.

He signed off his email asking me to have dinner with him
at the same restaurant where he'd advised me not to embarrass
myself by speaking.

Was Tom a fan of beach novels? *So not.* Nonetheless, he was asking, "What if?" about me. By his logic, when God ended a life, He opened a widow.

The story of Ron, my next major boyfriend, began in the purple-hazy offices of *High Times* magazine, the monthly rag for stoners and hydroponic gardeners.

Fashion magazine covers show a glamour shot of a model. The cover of *High Times* featured a close-up photo of a delectable, sticky, juicy, hairy bud of weed. Pot porn. The magazine was full of it: close-ups of plants and piles of herb either alone or strewn across the bodies of hippy chicks in crochet bikinis. After I was thrown out of *NYW,* my pal Violet hooked me up with some freelance work at *High Times.* She was the managing editor. Ironically, Violet was not, even back in high school, a pot lover. She was the only non-stoned person on staff. The rest of the editors lit up—right there, in the Midtown offices—as soon as they stumbled in the door at noon. And they didn't stop smoking . . . well, they didn't stop smoking.

It was a miracle the magazine ever came out. The editorial meetings started at point A and then meandered aimlessly, indecisively, all over the alphabet until Chinese takeout arrived. I copy-edited a few of the monthly columns, including the letters page. Readers would send in their personal anecdotes about smoking some awesome bud, their minds blowing wide open, the ensuing high-larious high-jinx. ("I can't believe I drove right off a cliff!") It was *Penthouse* Forum for freaks. Along with writing dirty anecdotes and profiles for *Climax* and *Playgirl* (until you've written porn, you haven't written at all), editing at *High Times* kept me solvent while I finished my first mystery novel and searched for a job at a "real" magazine.

Ron came by the *High Times* office one afternoon to visit a friend of his, a punk named Eric who edited the music section. We were briefly introduced, and then I went back to deciphering a reader's letter written in crayon on a crumpled cocktail napkin.

The next day, Violet said, "Here's the thing. That guy Ron who came in yesterday?"

"Who?" I asked.

"Eric's friend," she said. "Boots, leather jacket."

"Drawing a blank," I said.

"How quickly they lose their short-term memory," she said.

"What about him?" I asked.

"He thinks you're hot," she said.

I agreed to be fixed up. I'd logged a handful of one- or two-night stands in the year since Tom and I broke up. Might as well check out this Ron. What did I have to lose?

He turned out to be cuter than I remembered. A gritty Lower East Sider, he lived in a tiny one-bedroom apartment on First Avenue and Eleventh Street, behind an Italian bakery. Ron was a carpenter by trade, and had customized his place with a loft bed, an elevated platform for his desk (he called it "the command center"), and built-in shelving that made use of every inch of vertical space. The bathroom doubled as a watertight shower stall, like on a boat. Ron had rigged a collapsible rod and curtain to divide the space, and to keep the toilet dry when the shower was on. He kept his razor and toothbrush in a mug by the kitchen sink, which had a mirror behind it instead of a backsplash. His bike was sus-pended flat on the ceiling on four hooks. It was just so *neat*.

Despite the small space, Ron packed hundreds of tchotchkes on the custom shelving. Not porcelain figurines like you'd see at grandma's. He had a collection of '60s, '70s, and '80s rock memorabilia, sea glass (he grew up on the New Jersey shore), nostalgic kitsch, antique postcards. I was entranced by his stuff, what he'd built, the artistry and craftsmanship. I was incompe-tent at the simplest projects. At camp, my pottery had been lopsided. My macramé plant holder had looked like a lasso. My fascination with Ron's place wasn't only the "gee whiz" of a klutz who couldn't hammer a nail straight. Every corner told me who he was and what he could do.

The bed he made: a queen-size loft. It floated in the room. I floated on that bed. Ron and I had potent sexual chemistry. On our first date, we went to the Avenue A bar that became our second home. We drank. I smoked cigarettes. We made eyes at each other. Groped under the table. Went back to his place. After a year of screwing around with publishing types, I found Ron a welcome venture inside the toolbox. If I asked nicely, he would walk around the apartment wearing only his canvas work belt with the pockets and loops. He would strike "Men of the Carpenter's Union" calendar poses, hammer at the groin, an-gling up. Even more exciting, he would wear the belt, nude, to fix something. A wobbly chair. A loose shelf. Breakfast.

Physically, he wasn't a beefy works-with-his-hands hulk. He was five foot seven, only an inch taller than me, and slight. I probably outweighed him. But he was tight and perfectly in proportion, an immaculate dresser (combat boots, leather bomber jacket, T-shirts, and clean jeans). Green eyes, plump

red lips, long black lashes. At twenty-eight, Ron was prematurely graying, his hair cut short at the back and sides, a little
longer and curly on top, with sideburns.

The delight of my eye, Ron could also deliver a punch
line. His wit veered toward the crude. I hadn't realized how
many comic gems could be mined from farts, burps, queefs,
semen, vaginal fluid, boogers, and other effluvia. We chuck-
led up our lungs, Ron and me, over jokes that ended with jiz
in the face or poop in the pants. His friends, guys he'd known
since his days on the Jersey shore, wallowed in the nasty and
disgusting. For all I know, they were the trailblazers behind
Two Girls, One Cup. Ron's best friend theorized that you
could cook a hot dog inside a vagina, since a woman's body
temperature was 98.6. He asked Ron if he minded using
my mini-bake oven for the culinary experiment. Ron was
okay with it. (I declined.) None of his pals had a regular job.
They freelanced here and there, doing this or that, mooched
off/lived with their parents (no girlfriends), and survived by
extreme frugality. An evening's activity was often determined
by the number of crumpled dollar bills in their pockets.

Ron didn't have a job either. He worked sporadically,
whenever it came up. I was also unemployed and freelancing,
so who was I to judge? Our mutual flexible schedules meant
we could sleep in most mornings, Ron running to the bakery
downstairs in his pajamas, breakfast on the loft bed, afternoons
wandering the city.

Leaving the best for last: Ron could play the guitar. Really
play, not, as I could, strum a few three-chord Neil Young songs.
Hum a tune, and he could match it note for note on his classic
black Gibson electric guitar, the one item he possessed of in-

trinsic value. I could, and did, listen to him play for hours, then set his guitar aside, unzip his jeans, and admire his other sublime instrument. I urged him to start a band, make music his career.

"Not good enough," he said.

The first time? Bliss. Like we were the only people who'd ever had sex. On an early date, we were playing pool at a bar when he made a shot and I applauded. He came up behind me when it was my turn and whispered in my ear, giving me chills, "I adore you." He called constantly—so often, in fact, that I didn't have to worry about his next call. Our days were lazy. Our nights, full of passion and fart jokes. We fell into a habit of spending our time at his place. He tried a few nights in Brooklyn, but, alas, Ron was deathly allergic to my cat, Oatie. It was his one flaw.

Each year, to celebrate the tight cluster of January/February birthdays—mine, Howie's, and Dan's (now Steve's)—my parents took the whole family out to a three- or four-star Manhattan restaurant. (Thanks to this tradition, I've eaten at Petrossian, La Bernardin, Lutèce, Le Cirque, Bouley, Union Square Café, Gotham, Gramercy Tavern, among others.) The last time I invited a boyfriend was in college. So this time it would be a big step to bring Ron.

We got dressed up (he wore his only jacket and tie) and met my folks at Four Seasons. The introductions were smooth. The conversation was relaxed through the appetizer course. During the main course, the subject of cats came up. My sister, Alison, also a cat person, knew about Ron's allergy.

She said, "Just for the record, if you two get married, I'm not taking Oatie."

Ron almost choked on his Chateaubriand. Our future, after three months, had not been discussed. He didn't mention it, and for once, I kept my mouth shut, too. I had told my family and friends that Ron and I were serious, committed, in love. I *was* madly in love with him. But I hadn't told *him* yet. I was bursting to say it, though, and had planned to that very night after dinner.

On the taxi ride home, Ron was unusually quiet. Ordinarily, he'd have made jokes about crotch rot or anal itch. Back at his place, we sank onto the couch, stuffed.

I said, "Thank you for coming to the birthday dinner. It means a lot to me for you to meet my family."

Shifting, nervous, Ron said, "I liked them."

"Good," I said. "That's very important. That you like my family."

"I'm going to the bathroom."

He hid in there for twenty minutes. I sat three feet away. It wasn't like we couldn't hear each other. We'd carried on hundreds of conversations with one of us in the bathroom.

I waited for him to prepare for what was coming. He clearly needed to muster his courage.

He finally came out, and suggested we go to bed.

I said, "I love you."

"I'm crazy about you."

"Do you love me?"

He said, "I'm sorry, but I'm not there yet."

"Do you think you'll love me in the near future?"

"Maybe."

"When?" I asked. "Days? Weeks?"

"You'll be the first to know," he said.

I was wounded by this, but not mortally. I made two decisions: First, I was not a masochist who'd fish in a dry well forever. If Ron hadn't declared his love for me by June, six months hence, I was *out of there*! And he couldn't stop me. Second, I would back off, give him the necessary space to sort out his feelings and realize that, even if he couldn't admit it or didn't know it, he was already madly in love with me.

To make sure he didn't forget his homework (to-do list item number one: fall in love with Val), I prodded him with gentle reminders. I steamed the kitchen sink mirror and wrote a message with my fingertip that he'd discover after his next shower. "V + R" or "V loves R" or "R loves V????" Subtle stuff. I left notes—"Your eyes make me melt," "I love sucking your cock," etc.—tucked into the corners of his shelves, in his guitar strings, between plates, under the rug. (He must have been finding those notes for months after we broke up.) I rented romantic comedies and insisted we watch them on the couch, cuddled under a quilt. I noticed the look of horror on his face when I pulled out a box with John Cusack on the cover. I'd cry at the end, when the couple kissed. He'd jump up as soon as the credits rolled and circle his tiny apartment repeatedly, neurotically, like a caged animal.

By mid-February, I decided to press my advantage. I would later refer to this night as the Valentine's Day Massacre. My strategy was to overwhelm him, make it impossible for him not to say "I love you." Instead of writing a steam message on Monday, leaving a note on Tuesday, giving him a token of my love on Wednesday, etc., I would do it all, full strength, on one big night. I wrote in lipstick on the mirror. I bought him a gift, an effects pedal for his guitar. I handmade a card. The evening's entertainment (besides a new lingerie show): a special broadcast presentation of the most romantic comedy of all time, *The Princess Bride*.

Ron didn't have a gift for me. Or a card. He was angry about the lipstick on the mirror because it didn't come off easily. Also, he wanted to go out, not sit at home watching TV. His friends were going to the bar, and Ron wanted to meet them.

I insisted on the movie. Ron needed to see the allegorical story about true love. He sat there and watched it, unmoved. The last scene: Peter Falk closes the storybook and says to Fred Savage, "As you wish." I started bawling and said, "I love you. I want you to tell me you love me, too."

He said, "I'm attracted to you. But if I told you I loved you, I'd be lying."

The End.

Or, I should say, Almost The End. I bravely assured him that we needn't break up over his not loving me. We could continue as we were. Except, I took to crying whenever we had sex. A snivel a thrust. This was not a turn-on for Ron. His affection and attention dwindled. He used to call me every few hours, but was now down to a single ring. He made plans without me, was mysterious about what he was doing, which was usually going to the same bars with his friends.

Then he didn't call at all. Whether or not to call him was my only topic of conversation with friends during four agonizing days of sitting by the phone. America could have gone to war, I wouldn't have noticed. Everyone advised me to wait it out. I couldn't stand it, so I fled to my parents' house in

Short Hills for the weekend. Mom took me to see *Pretty Woman*. Not a great choice. Prematurely gray Richard Gere reminded me of Ron. A lamppost would have reminded me of Ron. I said to Mom, "Maybe if I were a hooker with a heart of gold, he would call."

By the end of the weekend, I'd reached the point of not-calling madness. I made one last-ditch effort to prompt him to call me. My friend Nancy was willing to do the dirty work.

She called Ron and said, "Have you seen Val? She was supposed to meet me and never showed up. I'm worried about her. Maybe she was in a car accident, or . . . she's been kind of depressed lately. You don't think she'd . . ."

If he thought I might . . . , he didn't call to find out. I phoned him later that night and told him I was fine, no car accidents or self-mutilation, on the off chance he cared. "You haven't called me in days. I can take a hint. Do you want to break up?"

"Let's be friends," he said.

As if!

I learned later he told his pals I broke up with him. Which, during the worst of my ditched grief, actually gave me hope. I wondered, *Did I?* Why would I do such a stupid thing? And could I take it back?

We got together a few times during our trial period of being friends. As soon as I saw him, I'd try to kiss him or take off his clothes. Once, I chased him around his apartment, got his pants down, and gave him a hand job, after which he thanked me and kicked me out. And I was so happy about it!

I went to Violet's apartment nearby and told her of my triumph. She looked at me like I was nuts, and asked, "What was in it for you?"

Good question. She could have been talking about the entire relationship with Ron, with Tom, and with several others.

I was addicted to feeling wanted. If I could get a man's attention, then I was desirable and worthy of love. I craved approval and adoration, and clung desperately to it. If a man started to retreat, I'd advance, wanting him more as he struggled to get away. It made no sense, never worked, and yet I repeated the pattern over and over again.

A confident woman knew her worth and could assess her relationship objectively. Was she happy? Did the guy satisfy her needs? Was she having fun? If not, she'd end it and move on. An insecure woman (me) thought every relationship, and every day in that relationship, was her last chance at love. When Ron and I broke up, I told friends, "I know I'll never love this way again," and not ironically. I believed that if my relationships failed, it was because I'd failed to be lovable.

E very year or so, a magazine editor called to ask me to write an essay on the subject "Advice to My Younger Self" or "What I Know Now That I Wish I'd Known Way Back When," or what I called the "If Only" essay idea.

"If Only" was a gimmick, but as such things go, not a terrible one. Editors wanted the piece to be darkly confessional and thoughtful—but funny!

I would enthusiastically accept the assignment and promise to send some ideas ASAP. *This would be a snap for a former teenage junkie whore—but funny!* I'd think, and then get down to opening a file, composing a list of themes.

"If only I hadn't spent my entire life on a diet," I'd type. But that subject was huge, could fill a book, and was way longer than the thousand words allotted.

"If only I'd been hard to get. I wouldn't have driven away every guy who was attracted to me," I typed. I should have mastered the art of romantic detachment, the M.O. that worked so well for some of my friends and colleagues. They showed nothing, and got everything from their boyfriends. I gave everything, and was shown the door. If my younger self had had emotional detachment, I wouldn't have suffered so much in love.

I never wrote that essay, for one reason or another. A better assignment would take precedence. Procrastination. My subconscious probably held me back. It was true: My needy-greedy behavior brought me to romantic ruin. But aspiring to be detached, wishing to feel *less,* would have been a bigger mistake, and the wrong advice to give to my former self, and to readers.

I should have felt *more.*

Oh, there was plenty of trumped-up ecstasy and overdramatized despair. But what about anger? What about resentment? What about annoyance?

I side-stepped the hate again, not speaking up when I felt righteously pissed off. The big difference between hiding my anger as a teenager and meticulously squashing it as a young romantic? The initial impulse was for self-preservation, to maintain dignity. Later, though, when I swallowed my anger in the name of love, self-preservation had nothing to do with it. Where was the dignity in chasing Ron around his apartment, grabbing at his zipper?

I was afraid to show anger to Tom or Ron because I didn't want to come off badly. Everyone knew: Men don't like bitches.

So I tried to be whatever they wanted me to be. In Tom's case, a dainty, clean-shaven, slow-eating intellectual snob. In Ron's case, a slacker beer-chugger who laughed volcanically over diarrhea jokes. Both personae were a disguise, like the "Me, 12" poker face, but desperate. I changed myself for them, and these guys *still* didn't want me.

I'm probably giving them more credit than they deserved, but maybe Tom and Ron didn't fall in love with me because they sensed I was a phony. That something about the way I acted and reacted was a deception. My range of emotion was disconcertingly narrow. What kind of person would hesitate to say, "Shut up and fuck you," when her boyfriend likened her appetite to that of a professional wrestler? What lowly creature begged on her hands and knees for the love of a man who'd given his consent for his friend to heat a raw weenie in her cooch?

If I *had* railed at Tom and Ron, they might've seen me as a fully articulated woman, not an empty vessel needing to be filled. Maybe then they'd have fallen madly in love with the real me, and asked me to marry them.

Thank *God* they didn't.

For all my analysis of their words and actions, I never took a cold, hard, objective look at Tom or Ron and asked, "Would the love of my life really tell me to put down the fork before I hurt myself? Would he belch the alphabet before bed every night?"

With twenty/twenty hindsight, I see them now for who *they* really were. Tom was a callous, pompous nitpicker windbag. Ron was a man-child who lived in a toy box, squandering his talent to swap adult diaper jokes with his stunted friends.

I'd been head over heels with these jerks. I'd obsessed over them, done some pretty intimate acts with them, wailed missing them, ached for them, would've given my right kidney for just one more night with them.

Love them? I didn't even *like* them.

Five

. . . .

Hate Your Way to Happiness

How many emotions *were* there, anyway? Hundreds? Thousands? Millions?

According to Robert Plutchik, the recently deceased psychologist and former professor emeritus at Albert Einstein College of Medicine, there are thirty-two. He organized them on his "Wheel of Emotions," a chart of the eight basic emotions, eight advanced emotions, and sixteen component varieties. The basic emotions come in pairs of opposites. Here are a few of them:

> *Joy and sadness*
> *Anger and fear*
> *Trust and disgust*

He classified advanced emotions in pairs of opposites, too:

Love and remorse (chew on that one for a minute)
Optimism and disappointment
Submission and contempt

The sixteen component emotions fill in the gaps between the pairs of opposites above. A sampling: serenity, ecstasy, acceptance, admiration, terror, amazement, pensiveness, grief, loathing (old friend!), annoyance, rage, and vigilance.

Each emotion on the wheel has a corresponding color. Sadness and grief, for example, are shades of blue (duh). Anger and rage? Red. Joy and serenity are sunny yellows. Fear and terror are lost-in-the-forest greens. Boredom and disgust are, bafflingly, hues of lavender.

Plutchik, a pioneer of psychoevolutionary theory, believed that the eight basic emotions evolved in all animals, including humans, as survival aids. Fear, for example, inspired our troglodyte ancestors to flee from sabertooth tigers. Fear protects New Yorkers from stumbling drunk into a dark alley at 2:00 AM. It keeps birds off the railing of our deck when the cats are prowling. When thuggish squirrels are on the deck, fear keeps our cats cowering indoors (pussies).

Of course, I was familiar with all thirty-two emotions. I'd traveled along each spoke of the wheel, from apprehension to pensiveness, disgust to acceptance. I'd felt annoyance, contempt, and disapproval so many times, it was as if the Wheel of Emotions had rolled over me, backed up, and run me down again.

But I didn't contemplate my emotions deeply, not even the juicy ones, such as love and regret. I knew I *felt* them. When

I looked at my daughters' faces, my heart burst with adoration. When a rival's novel made the *New York Times* bestseller list, I burned in a pit of jealousy. I thought that having the emotion was enough to understand it. But, in fact, experience only scratched the surface. If I was to become the master of my rage instead of being anger's prison bitch, I had to take my emotional consciousness to new heights. Or depths, as it were.

As far back as I could remember, I'd always been shallow, drawn to the bright and shiny, as opposed to, like my sister, the nuanced and subtle. When I was six and Alison was seven, our parents bought stuffed bunny rabbits for us as gifts. They were identical, except for the fabric of their jumpers. One wore a red-and-blue polka dot pattern; the other, a plaid of pink and green.

Mom propped the two toys next to each other on the kitchen table and said, "I'm going to count to three, and then run to the rabbit you like best. One . . . two . . . *three!*"

I dashed with a mad lust for the bunny in the primary colored spots. Alison went straight for the bunny in the pastel tartan.

Mom laughed and said, "I knew it."

Alison liked the visually challenging intricate plaid. I went for the simplistic, doltish dots. It seemed like Mom had orchestrated this rabbit test, if you will, to reinforce her previously held opinion about us. By first grade, I'd figured out that Alison was the smart sister. My brother, Jon—who proved to be a bona fide off-the-charts genius—taught himself to read at age four. And me? I was the pretty sister, until I got chubby. And then I was nothing but trouble.

A couple of months after my first colonoscopy, I went to Alison's house on Long Island for a Fourth of July barbecue. Burgers grilling, we paged through that week's J.Crew catalog. She dog-eared pages of print dresses and patterned blouses. I lusted for the metallic solids and jewel-tone tops.

"Do you remember that day Mom asked us to choose which rabbit toy we wanted? The plaid versus the dots?" I asked.

"Vaguely," said Alison.

"It was Mom's version of an IQ test," I said.

She shrugged, not buying it. "You can't attach that much significance to preferring basic versus complicated patterns."

Oh, *really*? I believed you could attach all kinds of significance to patterns—of fabric, behavior, or thoughts. I, for one, had a dyed-in-the-wool pattern of gravitating toward the uncomplicated, the easy. Book shopping, while Alison invariably picked up a weighty historical biography, I'd be at the New Paperback Fiction table thumbing a pulpy thriller or chick-lit novel.

"You do willfully skip over difficult emotions," Alison admitted at the grill. "You're fiercely determined to be happy. You've conditioned yourself to gloss over or forget anything bad. You refuse to reflect, or to let yourself experience pain."

"Remember the night Glenn died?" I asked.

Alison hated talking about it. She was there, with us. Glenn lay in the bed. I sat in the chair next to him, holding his hand through the guard rail. His fingernails had turned blue. Alison came into the hospital room. I updated her about what had happened in the last hour, that Glenn's breathing had become labored, erratic and that a nurse came in and gave him a heavy dose of morphine. I glanced at him, asleep, his breathing slower now. Alison asked what she could do. I didn't know. I looked again at Glenn and realized that his breathing, ragged only minutes ago, was quiet. Had stopped.

I blanked out the entire next hour. Arrangements and phone calls were made, by Alison, I guess. She drove me to her house (where we were now grilling burgers in the sun). Maggie and Lucy were already there, in bed, asleep. I crawled into the guest room bed fully dressed, passed out, and didn't rouse myself for twenty-four hours. I had to be shaken awake to go to Glenn's funeral.

Alison said, "What about it?"

"I remember that I had pain, but I don't remember what the pain itself felt like," I said.

"That's what I mean by being willfully happy. You have the ability to switch off the negative. You're lucky," she said, "but limited."

Back in Brooklyn the next day, I went to my friend Rebecca's brownstone in Cobble Hill—a ten-minute walk—for an evening snort of white wine. We sat on her stoop sweating like our iced glasses. Rebecca weighed in on my alleged superficiality. "You're definitely lowbrow"—referring to my love of *People* magazine, reality TV, and Ben Stiller movies— "but not necessarily lightweight. I'd sooner call you 'deluded' than 'shallow.' Like how you think Steve is a dead ringer for Daniel Craig."

"He is!" I said. Seriously, they look *exactly* alike.

"Like how you think your novels are the funniest books published in the last hundred years," she continued. "If you were shallow, you wouldn't be open to the possibility that you're deluded."

Did that make me deeply deluded? I wondered. If so, that was a step up from shallow. Or down.

Lots of shallow people take pride in their limitations, as in "I'm no college grad-u-ate, but . . ." or "I know I'm just a half-term ex-governor from Alaska, but . . ." At the core of *other* shallow people, there is a depth of insecurity about how they are perceived. It bugged me that I wasn't taken seriously. My fault. I'd been chronically (one might say *notoriously*) motivated by pleasure. I loved sex, food, recreational drugs, laughing hard, rock concerts, running—anything that made my heart beat faster. I'd explored an ocean of physical sensation. Emotionally speaking, I was stranded in the shallow end of the pool.

Alison and Rebecca could walk into a roomful of people and immediately be taken seriously. I would attract a certain type of attention, but not a lot of respect. They had gravitas. I had "keeping it light."

Thinking it through, I saw that my shallowness and haterdom were inexorably linked. If I'd been braver about expressing/exposing my hate in my braces-and-tube-sock days, in my needy-greedy relationship days, maybe I'd be a deeper, happier person. And now? Was there any benefit, other than stress relief, to facing and embracing negative emotions?

A deep person would probably know.

The answer probably lay somewhere at the bottom of my psyche. But whenever I dove in to find it, I skipped along the surface. Had I been a deeper person, wouldn't I have gained valuable insight from my experiences, rather than simply survived them? I should've learned a profound lesson from

Glenn's death. It should have changed me, given me grace, a healthy perspective about dealing with the small grievances of life. A deep person wouldn't have wanted to throttle insufferable moms who stopped me on the street to brag about their five-year-old chess prodigies, or go Serena Williams on incompetent salespeople. ("I'd like to take this fucking camisole and shove it down your fucking throat!")

Socrates said, "The unexamined life is not worth living." I tried to think profound thoughts, but they were so boring. Was I even capable of going deep?

"I think so," said Steve. "Human intelligence is a tool, a shovel. The smarter you are, the deeper you can dig." My husband thought I was intelligent. Glad someone did.

Smart = deep. Deep = dark. If depth would make me smarter, I was all for it. But if it made me darker or depressed? No, thank you.

"An animal doesn't wrestle with existential angst," said Steve. "Do our cats care that they're shallow?" I turned to watch our black cat, Ed, snap himself on the snout with a hair elastic, shake it off, and then do it again. Safe to say he didn't fret about his emotional limitations. And Ed was the happiest creature I knew.

Steve romanticized depth and despondence. His idol, the morose German composer Gustav Mahler, was famously miserable. "Mahler's music paints a vivid picture of sorrow and hopelessness. He couldn't have composed it if he hadn't been personally miserable," said Steve. Depth, misery, and artistic genius were historically connected. Van Gogh. Plath. Hemingway. Cobain. "I wouldn't trade happiness for any amount of fame or accomplishment," said Steve, a musician. "If I could take a pill to experience what Mahler felt for a few hours, I might try it. But I wouldn't want to live that way."

Me, neither. If misery were required for depth, I'd rather be a lesser artist. In fact, I *was* a lesser artist.

I called Lynn, who always had a sensible comment. "You want to be deeper? Why?" she asked.

For *more,* of course. To understand more, feel more, to get to the bottom, metaphorically, of what would make me happy and healthy long term.

"If happiness is a goal," said Lynn, "I'm not sure depth is the answer. Everyone I know who has depth spends a lot of time brooding about what's wrong with them, how they've failed, their setbacks. Thinking can be overrated." (Take that, Socrates.)

Not thinking *had* helped me during the lowest point in my life—grieving for Glenn. Compared with some of the widows and widowers I got to know, I mourned in a shallow way. The deep-style mourners tended to disappear into dark rooms, ignore their mundane existence, obsess about guilt and regret, and ask, "Why me?" The shallow mourners suffered, of course. They—we—cried, spent hours in pain. And then we went to the supermarket because the kids needed dinner. We didn't ask questions about the cosmic unfairness, religion, salvation. We suffered in uncomplicated sadness, and asked, "Why *not* me?" To Maggie, then five, and Lucy, then two, I said, "Life goes on for the living." So we went on living. Holding my family together during the year after Glenn's death was the one period of my life when I was taken seriously—but not because of what I thought, felt, or said. I didn't start spouting Kierkegaard or anything crazy like that. I coped. I carried on.

I got up, made breakfast, took the kids to school, and started writing again—*The Accidental Virgin,* a novel of romantic misadventure, for which I got no respect, needless to say.

A t life's crossroads—between books and marriages, and in the midst of philosophical and health crises—I visited my psychic friend Mary T. Browne. We met sixteen years ago when I worked at *Mademoiselle* magazine. Among other duties, I covered the New Age beat, i.e., psychics, astrologers, past-life regressionists, hypnotists, numerologists. Any subject matter that would make your grumpy uncle say, "Bull crap," I was in charge of. During that time, I learned about transits of luck-bringer Jupiter and taskmaster Saturn. I was fortunate enough to meet and write about famous psychics, including Char and Laura Day—and Mary T. Browne.

Believe what you will about Mary T.'s abilities and the dimension her insights come from. In this dimension, Mary T. was a trustworthy and dependable friend. She supported me with supreme generosity during Glenn's illness and death. A champion of Steve, she predicted our future happiness when everyone else said our relationship had started too soon after Glenn died (ten months) and would never last (eight years and counting . . .). As a psychic adviser, Mary T. guides people through the mist of their confusion. She made more sense to me than shrinks or rabbis ever had.

Which brought me to her Manhattan apartment that August afternoon for a chat. When I arrived, Mary T. was, as usual, in full makeup, with perfectly smooth hair, and was dressed way up, dripping jewelry, in a silk sheath and high(er than I'd try on) heels.

I sat down on the velvet couch in her cozy living room, taking comfort in the warm tones, oil paintings, and Tiffany lamps. She sat in a worn leather armchair facing me.

"So," she asked, getting down to it. "What's going on?"

I filled her in about the Lynch syndrome business. I hoped she'd look into my future and see a clean bill of health. I also described my increasing anger levels and general free-floating impatience and frustration with everything and everyone.

"Maybe it's a midlife crisis," I said, laughing self-consciously. "I just feel unsettled lately."

She focused her ethereal blue eyes on me. "Unsettled? Is that really it?" she asked. "You've worked hard, supported your family. You thought your life would get easier, but it seems to be getting harder. You're facing a health crisis, a career setback. What you're feeling is disappointment and disillusionment. Like 'Is that all there is?'"

I blinked with shameful recognition. She got all that in five minutes? Whenever I sat down with Mary T., it was like being naked in the room—with her fully, elegantly, dressed.

She was right. I *was* disappointed and disillusioned, over not only the crumbling of my rock-solid family genes but also my stalled career and my anemic social life, to say nothing of our faltering nation, the dismal economy.

"'Is that all there is?' sounds so greedy," I said. "I have two beautiful kids, a loving husband, some savings, a nice apartment. I should be happy with what I've got."

"You can't possibly be happy all the time, no matter how fortunate you might be," said Mary T. "And sometimes you have good reason to be unhappy. Having negative thoughts isn't something to feel guilt about. It's facing the facts of your situation."

"Negative thoughts and emotions won't come and get me in my sleep?" I asked. "That what *The Secret* and Rhonda Byrne would have us believe."

Scoffing at that, she said, "Everyone wants the easy fix. They're bewitched by the idea that there is an easy road to harmony and happiness. But the truth is, it's hard to be happy! People are complicated, and things go wrong. We have physical frailties, restless spirits, souls to fill. We're constantly facing physical and emotional challenges. But these challenges are karmic gifts. They give us the opportunity to master our thoughts, to understand ourselves better. Suppressing emotion is the antithesis of advancement," she continued. "You become a prisoner of your own emotions. You won't progress on your journey."

I bit my lip when she said *journey*. It's hard not to hate that word. Made me think of Steve Perry in zebra-print nut crushers.

I said, "I think I get it."

"Be emotionally authentic. Close the gap between who you think you should be and who you really are," she said. "If you're honest about your feelings, you're in harmony. If you're dishonest about them, you're in chaos."

Hard science backed up that concept. I'd recently read about a Canadian study where researchers asked subjects to write about their feelings and then, every fifteen seconds, when they heard a bell, to stop writing and say to themselves, "I am lovable." By the end of four minutes—and sixteen lightning-round affirmations—the subjects who'd tested low on self-esteem at the beginning of the experiment were in even worse shape by the end. The researchers concluded that the subjects' internal bullshit detectors were harsh contrarians. If you believed you weren't lovable, telling yourself otherwise only underscored your dismal opinion of yourself.

"These hiccups in life, like the one you're having now, they can be destructive and knock you off your feet," said Mary T. "Or they can be constructive and inspire you. Even if you don't have positive thoughts, you can take action. Use your negative emotions."

"To do what?" I asked.

She looked at me as if I'd just woken up from a nap. "To kick ass, Val."

I had to laugh. In her upbeat voice, Mary T. made kicking ass sound cute and wholesome, as well as karmically friendly. If ever there was a ringing endorsement of hating your way to happiness, this was it.

We continued our talk at Elephant and Castle, a café around the corner. I rehashed some of the stuff I'd been thinking about, my emotionally inauthentic friendships and relationships in the past. Even in some healthy friendships, I had been loath to lodge direct complaints or criticisms. Most recently, a pal canceled on me for the third time. I told him, "Don't worry, no problem," but the truth was, I was upset, feeling particularly vulnerable lately about how few friends I had.

"Why didn't you tell him the truth?" Mary T. asked.

I said, "I don't want to seem desperate or whiney, or to come off badly."

"You fear a negative reaction in your personal life," she

observed. "But in your professional life, you really put yourself out there. That's a glaring contradiction."

"Overcompensation in public to make up for the inadequacies in my private life?" I asked. "Maybe my subconscious is trying to tell me something."

But what?

My expensive anti-wrinkle cream (vain, shallow) was a thick gunk. I had to massage it into my skin for maximum penetration, which sounded sexier than it was. I spent a minute or two every night before bed, rubbing. Tonight, I repeated the Mary T. prescription for harmony: "Close the gap between who you are and who you think you should be."

I am a closet hater. I think I should be out.

My thoughts ran in circles about how I'd gotten here, how to proceed. I saw the logic in Mary T.'s statement that repressing any emotion would torpedo my health and happiness. Expressing anger, jealousy, and resentment, as needed, was the only productive and salubrious prescription for my malaise. It had already worked. When I double-parked and blocked in my bitchy neighbor, I did feel a power surge.

Doctors, shrinks, and psychics are unanimous. Rx: unleash the inner hater. But welcoming negative emotions with open arms was frankly terrifying. Like releasing the Kracken on myself.

I stared at my face in the mirror, skin slick with cream, brows knit in confusion. I'd caption this portrait, "Me, 44," or "Still Clueless, After All These Years."

"*I am* an insomniac," I said. "*I think I should* take an Ambien."

Steve came into the closet. "Talking to yourself again?"

"Not getting through."

"Wait a while before you take the pill," he said, for only one reason I could think of. The distraction of physical pleasure had come to save me from emotional probing again.

I welcomed *that,* arms open, in a heartbeat.

Six

....

That's So Great!

Why I tormented myself by reading the *New York Times* Sunday Book Review, I had no idea. It always made me insane with jealousy. This week in September was no exception. Right there, on page four, a rhapsodic review—might as well have been titled, "Buy This Book Immediately"—by impossible-to-please Janet Maslin, of a first novel by a writer named Yvonne.

I knew her, superficially (but of course). She was a stay-at-home mother at my daughters' school who, in her spare minutes, had been writing a novel for the last ten years. As organizer of the Mom's Book Club (which I never joined, since that would have meant leaving my apartment and talking to people on a regular basis), Yvonne once selected one of my books, which I appreciated heartily. When I saw her at school functions, she often asked me about my writing routine, some tips and tricks, how I'd managed to scratch out a career in publishing. Since I knew she was struggling to finish her book, I served to her this bromide: "The difference between a published novelist and an unpublished novelist is that a published novelist has written a book."

I already knew she'd finally finished hers. At a party about six months ago, our mutual friend Sarah told me the broad-strokes story of Yvonne's landing an agent and getting a book deal—major publisher, "significant" money, foreign rights sold around the world. I listened to the news, nodding, ooh-ahhing, smiling. "That's so great!" I said. "I'm so happy for her! She totally deserves it!"

Steve, who'd heard this conversation, told me later, "You must have said 'that's so great' twenty times."

And now her book was out, in a big way. A few more clicks of the mouse, and I discovered that Yvonne's novel was already a bestseller on Amazon. Barnes and Noble had picked it for their "Discover New Writers" program. Indiebound, a collective of independent booksellers, had made it their number one pick for the month.

Steve came into the office looking for a stapler. I said, "Check it out," and showed him the *Times* book review. "This is that woman from that time."

"Oh," he said. And then, "Who?"

I jogged his memory. "It's insane how jealous I am," I said.

Steve said, "There, there, Val. You'll feel much better if you use your negative emotions to take positive action."

He dared mock the wisdom of Mary T. Browne? There would be a hefty karmic price to pay for that.

"Shut up and fuck you," I replied (a clear sign of progress).

Groaning, I realized with a jolt that I'd RSVP'd "yes" weeks ago to Yvonne's Brooklyn bookstore reading/signing.

I searched my in-box for the date of the event. A month hence. The only way to get through that would be to hide in the corner to avoid catty mothers (I was thinking of two in particular) who might ask, "So, Val, has Janet Maslin reviewed any of *your* books?"

To which I'd reply, "Gee, no. In my wettest dreams, no. And it would never happen, not if Janet Maslin and I both lived to be a thousand years old."

The blood rush of jealousy sloshed in my ears, burned my throat, blackened my heart. This might be the hardest variation on hate to master. Would I ever? I hoped so, and quickly, or Yvonne's triumphant book event might make me pull out *all* my hair, and not just the little pile on my desk now, next to the puddle of my tears.

Yvonne deserved it! I was so freaking *happy* for her! This was so GREAT!

Honestly, her book did sound like something I'd love to read. If it had been a sleepy little rollout, I'd have been first in line to buy a copy. I'd have plugged her novel on my blog—with pictures and links. But now that it was an unqualified hit? I was too seething with jealousy to consider it. This glowing hand job of a book review had ruined everything!

It was hard not to hate Janet Maslin. There, I've said it.

The German word *schadenfreude* means "taking joy in another person's misery."

This wasn't my problem. I didn't celebrate another person's downfall—especially not another author's. What was good for one author, I believed, was good for all. A rising tide—Stephanie

Meyer, Sophie Kinsella, Dan Brown—floated all of our boats. I loathed seeing authors, publishers, any aspect of the book business repudiated. When disgraced pseudo-memoirist James Frey was flayed on *Oprah,* I squirmed in sympathy for him.

My problem was schadenfreude in reverse. I took misery in another person's joy.

Call it freudeschaden.

Don't bother looking it up on dictionary.com. You won't find it there. I made it up, but I didn't invent the condition. At lunch in a sandwich shop recently, I overheard two women— colleagues in the same office, apparently—begrudging the promotion of one of their peers. "I hate it that I'm jealous and competitive," said one.

The other said, "Me, too!"

"What's *wrong* with us?" asked the first. "We should be *happy* for Suzy."

And then they both started laughing at the ridiculousness.

The rich, the thin, the beautiful—I had no beef with them. If the world's wealthiest, most slender and gorgeous woman walked into my office this minute and asked for a cup of coffee, I'd give it to her. But if this woman said, "My first novel has just hit the *New York Times* bestsellers list"?

Hate. She could go get a cup of coffee in hell.

Back in high school, I didn't earn praise for my prowess on the sports field. I certainly wasn't winning any beauty contests. I had few friends, no boyfriends, was inept at art, music, math, foreign languages. I was voted "most likely to get stoned at a Clash concert." No one expected me to have a bright future. My own parents were afraid I'd get pregnant or drop out before I graduated.

The only thing I had going for me was the ability to string sentences together in a coherent and lively fashion. My siblings, same thing. Alison is also a journalist and author. Jon's first job out of college was at a daily newspaper. They had other talents. Alison excelled in every subject. Jon did, too, and he was a good athlete. Accolades came my way for one reason only. Although I nearly flunked trigonometry and Spanish, I breezed through English and history. If my grade depended on essay writing, I got an A.

I was talented at something I loved doing. A blessing. That I'd made a career of it? Bonus! Surely, that would be enough to satisfy a deep, secure, and emotionally authentic person. But as a shallow, insecure rage-aholic? I wanted more.

At lunch once, a wise editor told me a story about her bitter rivalry with a colleague. "A lot of bookish types—like me and you—didn't compete in sports or for popularity in junior high," she said. "We didn't get the chance to dull our competitive edge back then, so we're twice as ruthless now that we're adults. In the professional realm, it's easy to keep score—the bigger salary or job title wins. I scrape and claw for my victories, and feel tremendous satisfaction when I beat out _____ for a promotion. If you knew what a mouse I was in junior high, you'd be shocked to see me now in a meeting."

Did every motivation in adulthood originate in adolescence? Teenage losers have a lot to prove. Picture the former fatty showing up at her reunion in a size-two dress, or the AV geek turned software billionaire arriving in a limo with a third wife. I had a "Take a look at me now, a-holes!" fantasy, by proxy. I'd sooner peel off my own skin than go to a high school reunion. But my former junior high tormenters—as well as the bosses who fired me, the boyfriends who dumped me—could go to a bookstore and see my novels lined up on the shelf. They could read my articles and find my picture in magazines. Someday, they would see my name on the *New York Times* bestseller list.

But not today.

O nce upon a time, I was the target of freudeschaden.
So long ago, I can barely remember.

I got my first book deal—for a mystery called *A Deadline for Murder*—when I was twenty-five. Around the same time, I was hired to be an editor at *Mademoiselle*. Most of the other editors in the articles department aspired to one day write a book. Zina, in particular, had literary dreams. She was considered the best writer on staff, crafting thoughtful essays that the bosses, and readers, praised.

Zina's office persona was the generous, supportive, big-hearted softie. She spoke in a babyish, high-pitched voice and piled on the qualifiers, as in "I read your ideas memo. If I had to say, and it's just my personal opinion, and only as far as I'm concerned, I guess I sort of halfway think that maybe . . ." By the time her thoughts trickled out, she'd diluted them to meaninglessness.

The niceness was an act. Inside her small-boned body, Zina housed a plus-size green-eyed hater. My publisher sent over a box of my hot-off-the-presses novel, and I gave a copy to everyone in the articles department. Zina read the book that night. The next day, she told Abby, another editor, "Val's book is *shit*. Complete and utter *shit*." Abby wasted no time sprinting in high heels to my office to tell me what Zina had said.

For once, Zina gave a pithy review. I would've expected something windier, like, "If I absolutely had to say what I really thought of Val's novel, not that I'd ever intend to discourage anyone, ever, in my whole life, I think, I guess, I believe that the story sort of, kind of, a wee tiny little bit, resembled a speck of what might possibly, in some cultures, be considered *shit*."

As upsetting as Zina's trashing me behind my back was, Abby's ten-yard hallway dash to secondhand slap me—under the guise of "you should know"—was worse. Abby studied my reaction closely, greedily. My poker face failed me that time. I was humiliated, deflated, crushed, and I must have looked it. Abby smiled, seemed satisfied. She'd brought me low. Her work was done.

Did I defend myself? Speak up and say, "Zina's jealous, and you, Abby, are just plain mean?"

No way! Haven't you been paying attention? I bit my lip, my inner cheek. I would have gnawed off my fingers if necessary. After that momentary slip, I acted as if the criticism was as easy to brush off my shoulders as dandruff.

Zina's "shit" sandwich? I swallowed it whole. She came to my office later and said, "I loved your book!"

I beamed at her, and said, "Thanks ever so much. Coming from you, that means a lot."

What a relief it must have been for Zina and Abby when *A Deadline for Murder* earned mixed reviews (one described the book as having "all the pizzazz of stale popcorn") and sold pathetically. I didn't let failure stop me, though. Writing mysteries was my joy, gave me jollies.

If only joy and jollies paid the rent.

My book editor, Dana, told me to be patient. "It takes a while to establish a series," he said. "We'll give it four books and see if it catches on." Hard as I tried, my chain-smoking, booze-swilling saucy chick P.I. main character did not find an audience.

In my next incarnation as a novelist, I wrote stories about young urban women who stumbled comically and painfully into self-awareness and were rewarded in the end with romantic love. This type of tale became known as "chick lit." My novels, on the graphically sexy side, better fit the subcategory of "clit lit." I wrote six of them. I spent many happy hours laughing at my own jokes in my home office. A few of those titles were strong sellers. But, eventually, readers moved on. So I did, too.

Mysteries and chick lit exhausted, I proceeded to write a series of four novels for teenage girls, perhaps the purest pleasure I'd had yet in fiction. The *Fringe Girl* books sold approximately fifteen copies. I could've made photocopies, passed them out on the street, and done better. Next, I ghosted a novel for a pair of excellent broads, and wished I could say more about it, but was contractually forbidden. I wrote a "women's fiction" novel about ambivalent working mothers in shaky marriages—but funny! On the nonfiction front, I co-authored two self-help books (heartbreak and office politics) and three guidebooks (fashion, sex, plastic surgery). Last out of the gate was my first memoir about body image, of which I was quite proud.

Thus far, I'd written 22 books. I am currently working on number 23, a memoir. (You're soaking it in right now!) On average, that was 1.2 books—as well as 7 to 12 magazine articles—every year, for the last 20 years.

No one could accuse me of slacking off. Or giving up. I'd received five-star reviews, three stars, zero stars. I'd been sent fan mail from readers who gushed poetically, and hate mail from people who demanded their money back. I'd won an award and been nominated for others. My books had been translated into dozens of languages, all the predictable ones and some exotic, such as Turkish, Bulgarian, and Hebrew. I'd been published on every continent on the planet (except Antarctica; still holding out hope for the penguin).

And yet, I was as anonymous an author as Gertrude M. Sneedermann. Who? Never heard of her?

Exactly.

My largest successes were puny compared to the wild, unstoppable, raging whitecapped river force of, say, Candace Bushnell or Elizabeth Gilbert, two mega bestsellers who, *just like me,* started their careers as magazine writers in New York in the 1990s. I've never made it—"it" being, as any author could tell you, the *New York Times* bestseller list. My career has been defined by near hits as much as near misses. The movie based on *The Accidental Virgin*? Hasn't happened (yet), despite years of almosts. A TV series based on *Smart vs. Pretty*? Barely got a toenail off the ground. A Hollywood producer recently purchased the movie and TV rights for *Fringe Girl.* The story about two sisters in Brooklyn Heights was inspired by Maggie and Lucy. I wrote it for and about them, and would gladly have stuck with those characters in perpetuity, if that had been remotely financially feasible (so not). Seeing *Fringe Girl* come to life on the big or small screen would have been profoundly gratifying, a dream come true, the ultimate testament to my commitment as a writer and mother.

Naturally: Not. Holding. Breath.

I'd been just lucky enough, had worked furiously and adequately enough, to support my family modestly as a writer. (Neither of my husbands were rich, alas. I married twice for love. If there was a next time, as God was my witness, I was going for money.) I still scrambled to get magazine assignments and book contracts. I fretted constantly about my bank balance. My spirits rose and fell on my online sales ranking and royalty statements. My mood and livelihood hinged on factors beyond my control. I was envious of people with regular jobs, regular paychecks. Only as bankable as my last book, I knew that my dreams and ambitions put the security of the people who depended on me at risk. I had no guarantee of earning a consistent annual income, let alone another single dime. Job security? An illusion, even for authors who'd had bestsellers.

Writing wasn't a career *choice*. This was the *only* career I'd ever wanted, or had any hope of being good at. When I started out, yeah, I fantasized about striking it big. I still do. Dreams of literary stardom didn't die or fade away. They limped along, dragging tirelessly, like zombies.

When I lectured at New York University's graduate school for journalism, the students asked about cushy magazine editing jobs and lucrative writer contracts. Those gigs didn't really exist anymore, but the legend lived on. I asked the students if they were pursuing a career in publishing for the money, because, if that was their goal, they should quit right now and go to law school. A few of them admitted that they had applied to law schools for the upcoming year. I thought, "Good. Less competition."

I was fortunate that writing itself wasn't painful for me, as it was for many of my friends. I *loved* filling blank pages. I thoroughly enjoyed plotting stories, inventing dialogue.

Writing was easy. Making a living was hard. Making "it" was practically impossible.

A first-time novelist sent me an email asking me to "blurb" her, or supply a quote in praise of her book that would appear on the back cover. She'd been a fan of my work for many, many (so many) years. She remembered reading my articles in *Mademoiselle* when she was a toddler, barely out of diapers. I agreed to read the manuscript. I liked it, blurbed it, felt smug in my veteran benevolence and a trifle worried how the dewy-eyed novice would react when her debut failed to catch fire with readers. A few months later, the book came out, became an instant hit, a *New York Times* bestseller, readers lapping up more copies in a single week than my last five novels combined. Which, granted, wasn't much.

This *exact* scenario happened to me *four times.*

When it did, yeah, I felt a little sorry for myself. I didn't hate the author per se. I hated the cosmos that allowed anyone to have so much so fast. I hated the guilt and shame of my jealousy. I should be thankful for my good fortune. And I was! But, on *some* days, the grateful feelings were trampled by the sinister ones.

Jealousy was child's play compared to doubt. Perhaps I

lacked the talent, the skill, the understanding of human nature, the luck, the finger on the pulse, the tongue to the zeitgeist, the emotional depth to connect with a large number of readers in a meaningful way.

My next-door neighbor, a famous shrink, once asked me what my professional goals were. I said, "To write a bestselling novel."

She said, "I once dreamed about writing a bestseller. But then I decided it was too shallow a goal."

Shallow! She was calling my name.

I begged to differ, though. My bestseller dreams weren't (only) money and ego driven. Like the Na'vi in *Avatar,* I wanted to link my nervous system with that of others. As a reader, I'd experienced profound emotional connections to stories and authors many times. I wanted to supply the vehicle by which readers were moved and felt a deep connection with a character, a story, an idea. Was that ego? Couldn't be. Entertaining people, linking lives, contributing to the culture (even the lowbrow) via the written word was a noble, meaningful goal.

If only I could do it on a larger scale. My fans—the few, the filthy; you know who you are—were loyal. They "got" my sense of humor, which, as I'd been informed by readers and reviewers who found it hard not to hate me, was crass and tasteless. What to do? Tone it down? Doff the madcap? Dial back the dirty jokes and cussing? To what aim? To produce predictable, cliché-ridden sentimental goo where the characters sob, grouphug, and say "I love you?" at the end? I'd rather boil in oil.

Decades of cycling between expectation and disappointment had taken a toll on my fortitude. Sometimes, I felt defeated.

But then I'd write a page or paragraph that made me laugh, and hope came sputtering back. Hope turned doubt into delusion.

Maybe I *would* make it. If it happened the day before the end, *fine*.

Meanwhile, when a 30-year-old author's first novel was turned into an HBO series produced by Sarah Jessica Parker, I'd continue gnashing my teeth to the gum.

I took a deep breath and outed the full extent of my jealousy to my family and friends.

"I'm jealous of everyone who makes more money than me," said one of my sisters-in-law.

"I have a hate list, too. Everyone on it is rich, stupid, and higher up the masthead than me," said one friend about colleagues she'd worked with during *their* rise to the top.

One fabulously successful friend said, "That's *it*? Jealousy is your secret shame? Jesus, I thought you had a body buried somewhere. I hate tons of people! More each year." He also said he knew that a lot of people hated him right back, which he took pride in. In his business (in every business?), being hated was a measure of success.

"I'm jealous *all the time!*" said *the* Joan Rivers, American icon, the most successful person I knew or would ever know. "Anyone who says they're not jealous is turning a blind eye to their true emotions—or lying."

Go, Joan! I thought.

It was hard not to love her.

Quick back story: Joan and I met when I auditioned to

collaborate on a book about plastic surgery with her. Incredibly, she hired me and we produced a definitive user's guide to one of Joan's favorite hobbies. Landing this job inspired some professional jealousy among my peers. At lunch with two other chick-lit authors, I told them about the Joan book, how cool and funny she was, how, during editing sessions, her butler served us coffee and cookies on a silver tray, the bags of QVC jewelry and makeup she'd given me. They stared at me with frozen smiles, said, "That's so great!" And I *knew*.

"Rodney Dangerfield said that you want your friends to be successful, but you always want to be a little bit more," continued Joan. "I want everyone to do well. I stand backstage and feel thrilled that my friend Kathy Griffin is getting laughs. I've known her for twenty years, and I'm delighted she's gotten where she is. At the same time, I want to do better. I want bigger, faster laughs.

"I do know people who can put blinders on, like horses, and run their own race. Of course, everyone is running her own race, but it's smart to know that twenty other people are running alongside you," she said. "If there's one job, I want to be the one to get it. I have friends, they call me and say, 'I just got a TV show,' and I say, 'I'm so fucking jealous, I'm going to kill myself.' That's my way of congratulating them. You have to say out loud that you're jealous to keep it from taking over. Pretending it's not there makes it more powerful. Jealousy is a survival instinct. Nothing to feel guilty about or ashamed of. It's a motivator. Anything that spurs you on is good."

I described the contents of this chapter to a group of women at a small dinner party. The host, a staff writer for the most influential newspaper in America, mentioned the name of a colleague. "I've been obsessed with her career for ten years," she confessed.

The rest of us were baffled. "Why *her*?" we asked in unison.

"She's Metro desk," she said. "It's been my dream to work Metro."

Inexplicable! The host worked for a hot section. Her articles frequently appeared on the paper's "most popular" list. Hers was a dream job with flexibility and amazing perks. Anyone in her right mind would have been jealous of her!

And yet she pined for the pothole beat. Made no sense to me.

My jealousy made no sense to one of the other women at the dinner. She kept saying, "You, Val? How many books have you written? And you're jealous? Really?"

Yes, *really.*

Steve, an, actor, opera singer, and French horn player, was in a ruthlessly competitive business. I asked if he was jealous of Philip Myers, the legendary first chair for the New York Philharmonic, arguably the top horn job in the world. Steve said, "Of course not! He's a huge talent. He deserves his spot."

It did seem silly for, say, an amateur playwright to be jealous of Shakespeare. Or a chick-lit author to feel bitter about Jane Austen's success. The role model for overly ambitious jealousy: Antonio Salieri, the Italian composer whose hatred for Mozart became his obsession and drove him to madness.

My brand of jealousy didn't take lunatic form. It was reserved for peers, meaning women of comparable ability and age who wrote in my genre(s). I was in awe of, not jealous of, writers of superior talent—of which there were so very many.

Any author who'd had a hardscrabble childhood was beyond the reach of jealousy. Who could begrudge Augusten Burroughs *anything* after what he'd been through?

I had a high tolerance for others' triumphs if they were humble. A guy in my neighborhood wrote bestselling novels, was nominated for an Oscar for best adapted screenplay, and directed critical and commercial hit movies. His other great talent was the ability to downplay. I ran into him at the gym the Monday after his new movie came in second at the box office.

"Congratulations," I said.

He smiled bashfully and said, "The only difference between last week and this week is that people are returning my calls. Who knows what next week will bring?"

I got the feeling that he had used the line before, knew it would have a soothing affect, and secretly puffed himself up by trampling down his glee. I didn't care. His downplay was a kindness. I liked him for it.

On the other hand, if he'd said, "I've got three more movies in development! Brad Pitt's on speed dial!" it would have been criminally unjustifiable—and of course, so very hard—not to hate his stinking guts.

Not all of the professionally fortunate bothered to downplay their success. Exhibit A: a nearly faithful copy of an email solicitation from a novelist sent to her Facebook friends. Most authors made announcements about their new books, and issued pleas for people to buy them. I did, apologetically. This writer took a different approach, as you'll see below. The emoticon, vainglory, pandering, failed attempt at irony, dreadful punctuation, and hubris were all hers.

That's right, everyone! Tomorrow is the big day you've all been waiting for: the paperback release of the New York Times best selling novel, *Sentimental Cliché*! **Oh, and guess what? I wrote it.** :) Because I am only friends and family with truly awesome, in-the-know people, I'm sure you must have heard that dozens of major media outlets—the list is so long, I hate to bore you—have raved about the book! My beloved amazon reviews—500 of them, luv you guys!—have given the book 4.5 stars! Even if you bought a hardcover version, I'm sending you **a big, fat, virtual kiss,** but will also **pretty, pretty please** ask you to get a paperback copy for any woman in your life you can think of, even people you haven't thought about in years (hello, facebook!), even a random person on the street, **whose life will be richer by reading this.** In all seriousness, I sincerely appreciate all of the support. Thanks again for all of your help making me an even bigger success than I already am. **I truly, honestly, totally appreciate each and every sale 100%!!!**

Could make a person sick, no? Once upon a time, I liked this woman. But then, *yeesh,* this steaming pile landed in my in-box.

From whence disgust? The sopping tone, the dual theme of sycophantic begging and shameless bragging. Steve read the email and said, "What's *wrong* with her?"

Her line "Oh, and guess what? I wrote it! :)" became a running gag (joke and dry heave) in our house. When I served dinner, I'd say, "Oh, and guess what? I cooked it!" After Steve tended to the litter box, he'd say, "Oh, and guess what? I scooped it!" Maybe her "awesome, in-the-know" friends *would* buy a hardcover, and then multiple paperbacks, for which she'd be, like, truly, in all seriousness, sincerely, honestly, *totally* appreciative, a hundred thousand million percent! With tons of big fat virtual kisses!!!!! And hugs!!!!!!!!!!!!

Me? I was offering blow jobs for book sales. And still, I got no takers.

This woman had made "it." She'd been on the *New York Times* bestseller list.

Oh, and guess the fuck *what*? I hadn't! :(

Rebecca refused to indulge me on this subject. "One of my favorite things about you, Val, is your confidence," she said. "You love your work. You think you're hilarious. So what if the whole world doesn't agree? When you talk about feeling jealous of horrible writers like _____, you sound pathetic."

She recently went to see memoirist Mary *The Liars' Club* Karr at Joe's Pub in Greenwich Village. "Karr is a bestseller who also wins literary prizes, who can fill a huge venue of paying customers just to hear her talk," said Rebecca. "And she was bitter about Sarah Palin's book sales. Everyone is looking up. Believe it or not, Val, a lot of writers are looking up *at you*. Even if you were as successful as you wanted to be, you'd find someone to be jealous of."

Maybe. I wasn't so sure. Fessing up, spending a couple of weeks talking nonstop about professional longing and freudeschaden really took the edge off it. Joan Rivers was right. To muffle jealousy, scream about it. If I'd known this years ago—all the clumps of hair and bitter tears I'd needlessly sacrificed! What a waste.

My agent called. That novel, the one about the overwhelmed moms in troubled marriages—but funny? A major publisher had made an offer. Hardly a "significant" deal, not even close. But it was (a little) more than I'd hoped for in the bizarro world of post-recession book publishing. After three years' absence from the New Fiction table, I would be back. The timing of the call—it felt like a reward for honesty. I'd confessed my rampant jealousy. In exchange, my luck would hold. There would be another book. Another year living the dream. Another chance.

I bought a new dress, a silver metallic ruffle sheath from J. Crew, and I debuted it at a midtown Greek restaurant for a celebratory lunch with my agent, Nancy, and my two new editors, Linda and my old pal Dana, the editor of my mystery series in the early 1990s. Together again, after all this time. We were both thrilled.

Linda said, "Should we order champagne?"

"Yeah, baby!" I said, just to be agreeable.

"Before I forget," said Linda. "I have gifts."

She reached into her tote. First, she pulled out a soon-to-be-published thriller by Jonathan Kellerman, one of my all-time favorite authors. I greedily grabbed it, smelled it, hugged it.

"This one," she pulled another book from her tote, "is a novel by a first-time author. It's doing really, really well for one of our imprints."

Yvonne's book, of course.

I groaned, loudly, dramatically. This was *my* lunch, God-damn it! Did jealousy have to intrude now?

"What, you don't like period fiction?" Linda asked.

"I know the author." I explained how I'd, embarrassingly, driveled out bombastic advice to her over the years. How generous and supportive she'd been about my books. How funny and sweet she was, how long and hard she'd worked on her novel. "I'm so jealous of her success," I said, "I could kill everyone in this restaurant."

My lunch dates? They *laughed*. They found my rank jealousy amusing. They *liked* me for it.

"Don't worry, Val. We'll just have to make sure your new novel is an even bigger hit," said Linda, which was exactly the right thing to say. It filled me with humility and gratitude, knowing full well that her words were unlikely to come true.

The even-keel feeling was tested, again, at Yvonne's book reading in Brooklyn in October. Of the hundreds of book parties, readings, signings, and events I'd been to over the years, none was as amply attended. Had to be two hundred people there! The place was *packed*. Bursting. Like the bubble of my goodwill.

Daryl met me there. A magazine book review editor who'd been to countless author events, she couldn't believe the turn-out either. "Who *are* all these people?" she asked, looking around in amazement.

Holy shit, I wondered with dread, *are they fans?*

Maybe a few. Yvonne took the lectern and thanked everyone for coming—her family, her friends, the students and mentors from her creative writing workshop, the ladies of her book club, her squash league, members of the parents association, the gardening club, the caroling club, former sorority sisters, her trainer, her grocer, her doctor, her neighbors—the list went on, and on, and *on*.

Not only would Yvonne join a club that would have her as a member. She'd join *any* club. No wonder it had taken her ten years to write her novel. She'd been busy gardening, playing squash, phone treeing, and caroling.

I was no longer jealous of Yvonne, at all, for her literary success. Re: her ability to make and maintain friends?

Oh, *yes*. Terribly.

I whispered to Daryl, "I have no friends."

She whispered back, "This woman would make Michelle Obama feel inadequate."

We agreed. It was regrettably, unfairly, terribly hard not to hate her. And I mean that in the nicest possible way.

Seven

....

How to Hate the Man You Love

Thanksgiving weekend, Tiger Woods drove into a tree, and the whole world was talking about lying, cheating, stinking garbage cans of bad husbands.

Any wife should hate a husband who is caught with a hooker (Eliot Spitzer, female; Ted Haggard, male), cheats with every stripper or Nazi pinup he meets (Tiger, Jesse James), is a codependent, unrepentant addict (Blake Fielder-Civil), lies about his identity (Christian Karl Gerhartsreiter, the "faux Rockefeller"), or plots murder to replace you with a younger model (Scott Peterson, Henry VIII).

Most of the dastardly deeds listed above were tabloid fodder, extraordinary cases, or celebrity malfeasance—rare among the hoi polloi. The following offenses, however, were committed by ordinary people whom I or my friends knew personally:

The husband who lost his job and decided that, since his wife did okay financially, he'd let her support him. He hadn't worked a day since the *last* recession, in 2001.

The hubby who gained a hundred pounds over ten years of marriage, despite his wife's fears for his health and her diminishing attraction to him. "If she doesn't love me the way I am," he said, "why should I give up Big Macs for her?"

The heart attack survivor with a horrible family history of cardiac arrest who refused to quit smoking, despite dire warnings from doctors and tearful begging from his wife. After he died at fifty, she said, "If he weren't dead, I would kill him."

A man who stopped having sex with his wife after a career setback. His libido, he said, was linked inextricably to his income. If he wasn't raking it in, he couldn't get it up. Until the economy recovered, he said, she'd just have to masturbate, which she'd been doing for two years and counting.

The husband who hated his wife's friends and family so much he hung up on them whenever they called.

The groom who lied to his bride about having an STD and gave her herpes. Her symptoms were so severe she couldn't risk having unaffected children.

The guy who took in his elderly parents and expected his stay-at-home wife to attend to their needs—cook, clean, entertain, dispense medications, drive them to doctors—while he did nothing to help.

The husband who trolled for dates online, both male and female, while his wife worked two jobs to support them.

The newlywed who slowly bled their joint savings account to maintain the yearlong fiction that his salary was double what he actually earned.

And the garden-variety obnoxious husbands . . .

Rabid sports fans.

Sloppy open-mouthed chewers.

Political nuts who preached for an hour about campaign finance reform.

Flirts who took it two steps too far at parties.

Weekend drinkers who didn't know how much was too much.

Shirkers who promised to repair the crack in the ceiling every weekend for five years.

Passive-aggressive types who regularly "forgot" to take out the trash, pick up milk, or do the dishes.

Selfish lovers who made insincere offers to "take care" of their wives after they were finished and half-asleep.

Tantrum throwers who stormed out of the house and returned an hour later sulking.

If you were to pick apart *any* boyfriend or husband, you could find flaws aplenty and excellent reasons to hate him— and you should! In a marriage, some anger is good. In fact, wives' lives depend on it. A well-reported psych study a few years back found that self-silencing wives who didn't express their anger and annoyance to their husbands were *four times more likely to die in a ten-year* period than their bitching, nagging, complaining counterparts.

Not hating your husband *could kill you.*

Elin "Nine Iron" Woods? She'd be fine.

I worried about Silda Spitzer.

I was a time-delayed self-silencer. When I got angry with my husband, I didn't swallow my anger. Well, maybe I did *at first.* But, mother bird–like, I'd regurgitate it later, all over him. After fretting about something he did or said for a day, or a week, or four years (the time Steve casually, *stupidly,* asked me to lose my belly fat), I'd eventually work up the courage and indignation to speak up about it, thereby *saving my life.*

Unfortunately, the bursting of the "God damn" usually occurred at 3:00 AM. I'd nudge Steve awake to say, "That thing that you said that time? I'm upset about it." Which was probably the number one thing Steve (and Glenn, for that matter) hated about me.

How did I hate Steve? I counted the ways. There were three:

Steve Disappeared

Steve loved beer. He'd marry beer if it could cook and had a vagina. When we first started dating, I found his beer knowledge quirky and impressive. Steve knew the difference— ingredients, age, flavor, color—between a pilsner, a stout, an ale, and a lager. Under the kitchen sink of his bachelor pad in Manhattan, he used to ferment his own hops and bottled the microbrew for himself and his friends. A connoisseur, Steve wouldn't drink cheap swill like Bud in cans. His sophisticated barley-hop palate delighted in freshly drawn pints from a tap, brim foamy, body nutty and bold, cold glass.

If Steve read that last paragraph, he'd be out the door already, on a quest to slake his thirst.

The beer jones struck a couple of times a week. He went to Pete's Waterfront Ale House, a pub on Atlantic Avenue in Brooklyn, sat at the bar with a book, usually a biography of a comedian, and drank. The seven-hundred-page Michael Palin memoir was good for an entire season on the stool. Depending on his frame of mind, Steve could be gone for twenty minutes or a few hours.

Was it beer he loved or getting away from me and the kids? Why couldn't he, I asked, escape soberly into a book, like I did, when he needed a break from family life? He'd rather vacate the premises and guzzle beer with a bunch of strangers (except the bartenders, whom he knew all too well).

Since he hardly ever got drunk-drunk, Steve didn't understand why I objected. Of course, it would be healthier for him to go to the gym than the bar, Steve readily agreed. But that was not going to happen. Every tap in every pub in all the world would run dry before Steve went to the gym.

"Got milk!" he said one night when he came home hours later than his dash to Key Food warranted. Meanwhile, the dinner I had prepared was already packed into Tupperware in the fridge.

I asked, "Where *were* you?" but I knew he'd been to the bottom of a few pint glasses. "You can't be more comfortable on a hard stool in a drafty, smelly bar than you are on a soft couch in your warm home."

He formulated a response. I waited, and waited. People from Maine think long and hard before they speak. Sometimes, while I waited for Steve to reply, he'd look up at me and ask, "What was the question?"

I repeated, "What is the appeal of Pete's?"

He said, "I needed to get out, be alone."

"In a bar full of people."

"Okay, 'alone' isn't exactly it. 'Away' is what I need. To go off by myself. It's like making a clean getaway. That's why I turn off my phone, and don't say when I'll be back. It's freedom for a few hours."

"Is this a man thing, slinking off to be a lone wolf when the moon is full, or half full, or not out yet?" I asked.

"No one's stopping you from going out," he said. "You should! Call Nancy or Rebecca. Go to a movie. Have a drink. It'll do you good."

"I don't *want* to get a drink on a Tuesday night at six PM," I explained. "That's not acceptable behavior for a mother when the kids need homework monitoring and a hot dinner. *Someone* has to be here. *Someone* has to be responsible, even if no one *else* appreciates it."

"You sound just like your mother," he said.

Oh, and I hated Steve with a white-hot passion when he compared me to my mom. Which he did, whenever he wanted me to shut up, regardless of whether or not he was right.

Steve Was Moody

FYI: Twenty-two percent of American wives currently out-earn their husbands, the highest percentage than ever before in our nation's history. Alpha wives, as we are called, put a ring on it, and we pay for it, too. Steve, a beta husband, worked just as hard as I did, practicing the horn for hours every day, rehearsing, performing, and touring with his opera company. But his income was small. When we married, the plan was that he'd pay his bills—health insurance, clothes, his cell phone, his *beer*. And I would pay for myself, the girls, and the apartment.

"So when you go on vacation, you pay for everything?" asked a friend once. "That'll get old real quick."

I was okay with it. I placed a tremendous value on what Steve brought to our relationship apart from cash. He did 75 percent of our household chores, listened to me puzzle through books and articles, hugged me, rubbed my back, did school pickup and art projects with the kids. He fixed the plumbing and caulked the shower. He made sweet, sweet love to me nearly every night (put a price on *that*). There was the not estimable value of his fatherhood to Maggie and Lucy. He legally adopted them two years ago, a complicated process that involved scores of documents, thousands of dollars, nearly a year of our time, home visits, interviews, lawyers, a judge in robes. We made it official at Brooklyn Family Court on Valentine's Day, aka Adoption Day, an easy anniversary to remember and celebrate.

I was more emotionally dependent on Steve than he was financially dependent on me. When we met, he was forty-seven, and had supported himself—zero debt—as a professional musician since he graduated from the New England Conservatory at twenty-two. He lived in a small apartment in Washington Heights, at the northern tip of Manhattan, ate a lot of pasta, and got discount tickets for shows and concerts through Actors' Equity and the musician's union. He traveled—on opera tours. He didn't crave material possessions or pine for riches and fame. He just wanted to play music. He was prepared to continue the starving artist lifestyle indefinitely, no regrets. He married me and moved in with us. Life got cushier. But Steve could make do with less, with next to nothing. I admired him for it.

A few years ago, he went home to Maine for his grandfather's funeral. Practically the whole town turned out to pay their respects. Steve saw people he hadn't thought about in decades, including Jay, a man who'd grown up on the same street and used to put firecrackers in anthills and once in the mouth of a frog. "A pre-psycho," Steve described him.

"Heard you got married," said Jay at the wake.

"Yup," said Steve.

"You still doing that opera stuff?" asked Jay.

"Yup."

"You make much money at it?"

Now, Mainers are fiercely private. This would normally be considered an offensively personal question, even if Steve's sisters or brothers had asked.

"Nope," said Steve. "Not getting rich, but I love what I do."

"I love hunting and fishing, but I can't do it every day," said Jay. "You've got to be a man, start supporting your family."

Jay worked for the town's municipal construction company as a digger. Steve told me, "It was the job that a lot of guys took after high school graduation if they weren't capable of doing anything else." I marveled, again, at how far Steve had come from the factory town in central Maine where he grew up, how much courage it must have taken for him to leave his family in the country to pursue an artist's life in the city. Of his six siblings, five of them still resided in Maine. Three lived within a few miles of the house they grew up in, which was half a mile from the house their grandparents lived in.

Neither Steve nor I cared what Jay thought about husbandly duties. Jay would have collapsed in shock if he'd known Steve did our family's laundry. And the vacuuming. As long as we could afford our lifestyle, Steve and I pledged to support each other in our careers, however risky and low paying. Ours was an unconventional marriage, but we were committed to it wholeheartedly.

The comment from Jay burrowed into Steve's pride nonetheless. He suspected Jay was parroting what he might've heard from Steve's traditional-values father and brothers. Steve always felt misunderstood by the other men in his family, a nagging ache from childhood.

When he came back to Brooklyn after the funeral, Steve sank into a bleak period that lasted a month. He was surly, grumpy; he went off sex, conversation, me, the kids. He'd come out of it and act normal for months. But periodic shorter depressions crept up, lasting a couple of days or a week. When he withdrew into a mood, the girls were hurt and mystified. I felt rejected and lonely. Our income discrepancy—pricing a vacation, shopping for a new TV, paying for a car repair—set him off nearly every time.

Everyone was entitled to the occasional mood, but I took Steve's personally. I tried to get him to open up and talk about it—"Do you think your father doesn't respect you?"—but the subject matter was too sensitive. His reticence frustrated me terribly. Which brings me to my next complaint:

Steve Didn't Engage

The self-silencing husbands in that marriage study did *not* die any faster than their expressive counterparts. But what about their wives? I can tell you: my blood pressure shot through the roof when Steve shut down. Was there anything more infuriating than a man who refused to discuss a problem in the relationship at 3:00 AM or otherwise?

After one spectacular fight, which consisted of my yelling Val Black style and Steve shaking his head in stony silence, I called Jane Greer, PhD, a friend, couples counselor, and reliable source. "How can I get him to open up?" I asked.

"Instead of accusatory 'you' sentences that start 'you always' or 'you never,' use 'I' sentences. 'I feel' or 'I think,'" she suggested. "And don't make statements. Ask questions. Pretend you're on *Jeopardy!*, and put everything in the form of a question." I made Steve get on the phone, too, just so he could hear the advice directly from Jane. If he got it from me, he might not take it seriously.

A few days later, Steve acted standoffish when we ran into a former colleague at Key Food. I said, "What is I feel like you can be such a prick sometimes?"

He replied, "What is I think you're overreacting?'"

"What is I wish I were?"

"What is I know you are?"

"What is let's just finish shopping and go home?"

"What is I want chicken for dinner?"

"What is I'd prefer pasta?"

Jane's strategies worked—though, maybe not in the way she meant. We weren't engaged in a productive conversation about our conflict. But we were laughing together, which, unlike fighting productively, we were very good at.

The night before I married Glenn, my mother sat me down on the couch in Short Hills (the same one I'd flung myself on during that epic seventh-grade mope session, and the one where she'd screeched, "She knows the lingo!") for a private pre-wedding talk. I was afraid she might tell me about the flashlight and the cave.

"I've got two bits of advice about marriage," she said. "First, there will be some things you never get over about your husband."

"So I should learn to accept them," I said.

"No. You'll *never* accept them," she said. "That's why it's hard."

"Okay," I said, believing that Glenn was perfect and would always be. That turned out to be false. I struggled with his indecisiveness and lack of confidence, as did he.

Mom continued: "Second, as long as you can look across the table at your husband and think, 'He's cute,' you'll be okay."

Glenn was totally cute! And Steve? God, yes! (I might already have mentioned his uncanny resemblance to a certain British actor.)

I asked, "You think Dad is cute?'"

"I do," said Mom.

Looking at my parents' black-and-white wedding photos— Judy was barely twenty, Howie was twenty-three—I was knocked back by how gorgeous they both were. Judy's makeup was precise and dewy, arched eyebrows, radiant skin, a breathtaking profile. Her hair: polished perfection. And her dress! White silken layers, tailored to cinch her impossibly tiny waist. I hadn't had a waist that small since I was five . . . months. Dad was rakish (Jewish version) in his tux, black tie undone, top shirt button open, a tipsy smirk on his clean-shaven, sharp-jawed face, one lock of shiny black hair dipping out of place across his strong brow.

And now? Five decades later? Usually, when a septuagenarian is described as cute, it is a condescending nod to their adorable decrepitude, as in, "Look at Grandpa trying to feed himself peas, but they keep falling off the fork. So *cute!*"

At seventy-three, Dad's jaw was softer than in his wedding photos. His brow had deep lines. He continued to grow luxurious, shiny black hair—out of his ears. Except for a bit of a paunch, he was still slim. Recently, we hiked seven miles along the New Jersey portion of the Appalachian Trail. Our group included the young (Maggie, Lucy, and cousin Lily), the middle-aged (me, Alison, and Lynn), and one senior, Howie. Despite his advanced age, Howie was among the first to finish.

Mom's "cute" wasn't only about physical appearance. She meant affectionate appreciation for his looks, yes, but also his wit, his charm, how animated he got when he talked about his passion. Howie's passion was rocks. He retired from medicine at sixty to get his master's in geology. He was downright cuddly when he gave impromptu lectures over dinner about shiest, Pangaea, Krakatoa. The kids and I teased him, pretending to doze off, snoring loudly, jerking awake. He laughed along.

What Mom never got over about Dad was his moodiness. He loved wine a little too much. He wasn't emotionally communicative. He disappeared into his garden for hours and hours . . . *hey, wait a minute!* No wonder Steve and Howie get along well. They had so much in common. And Mom and I shared the same frustrations. We both found our husbands' reticence and distancing hard not to hate.

I could understand why Howie shut down and felt compelled to escape from Judy. No matter how cute she could be across the table, Mom was often intense, edgy, neurotic, demanding, critical, and loud. A few hours of silence was little to ask of a fifty-year marriage. Dad just wanted peace.

Only six years into our marriage, Steve sought the same.

But I wasn't my mom—yet. Transformation to Val Black not yet complete. My occasional loudness probably did drive Steve to Pete's or into himself. It was probably healthy to tolerate his absences, even to support his leaving me, physically and emotionally, when he felt the need.

Jane Greer said, "You have to let him go away. Give him the chance to miss you, and feel excited about coming back." Otherwise, she warned, "he might not want to."

Steve didn't come with us when Howie, Judy, Alison, and I went to Major Cancer Center in Manhattan in mid-December. We'd had to wait months for our appointment with the expert gene team to talk about our Lynch syndrome mutation.

In the meantime, Alison had a colonoscopy. A polyp was found. It was a good size, with pre-abnormal cells (Stage -1?). Testing revealed the same microsatellite instability markers as in my polyp. The chain was unbreakable. A grandmother, father, and sibling with abnormal or precancerous growths, and an abundance of evidence of a gene mutation. We officially matched the Amsterdam criteria for a Lynch syndrome family.

As part of our pre-appointment prep, the Major Cancer Center counselor asked us to research our family health history, as far and wide as we could manage. Mom and Dad worked the phones, collecting info about Dad's extended family for generations. An uncle with bladder cancer. A great uncle with pancreatic. A cousin with colon. My grandmother had two bouts of colon, one uterine, and one ureter cancer. It seemed insane that no one had noticed our family's tendency to get early-onset cancers in the same body parts. Back in Grandma's day, Lynch syndrome was as yet undiscovered. Professor Henry Lynch coined the term in 1985. (It went by other names as well: cancer family syndrome and hereditary nonpolyposis colorectal cancer, or HNPCC.) The science of genetic research itself was in its infancy then. Unlike my older, deader relatives, I was forewarned and could take preventative measures. On the other hand, I had to live with the knowledge of what might happen.

"Based on your family history and tissue testing," said the genetic counselor, a fortyish woman with a Russian accent, "you are as close as we can get to a positive diagnosis." We were seated at a round table in a drab if clean conference room. The counselor had made a chart of our family tree, thanks to the info Mom and Dad had provided. Each member was represented by a square or circle (depending on gender), filled in black if he or she had had cancer. Dad's side of the tree? Blighted.

Much of the conversation went over my head: proteins, mutation markers, enzymes. I sat there dazed and itchy, wanting badly to leave. Alison felt the same way. About halfway through the meeting, she did flee to a business lunch, which was her legit excuse to get out of there.

After a while, the genetics doctor swept into the room: mid-fifties and slim, with wire-rim glasses, a bow tie, and an air of officiousness. He launched right into Major Cancer Center's sales pitch, not wasting a breath to quell our anxieties.

"I've gone over your history and pathology reports," he said, adjusting himself in his chair. "And I have recommendations for each of you."

He told Howie to get annual colonoscopies, endoscopies (of the esophagus, stomach, and small intestine) every three years, and yearly urine analysis to test for blood and/or abnormal cells in the kidneys, bladder, and area tubing.

Nothing for Mom. Her genes were clean.

Alison (I took notes for her) and I should follow the same screening schedule as Dad. But also our ovaries, uterus, and cervix should be surgically removed as soon as possible.

I'd had months to get used to this. I figured, give me an estrogen patch, leave me my vagina and clitoris (especially the clitoris), and I'll muddle through.

Bow Tie said directly to me, "Since you had colon cancer already, we recommend a prophylactic total colectomy," or surgical removal of my entire large intestine.

Didn't sink in. "Why do you keep saying I had cancer?" I asked. "I had *pre*cancer, like Alison and Howie."

"No," he said. "They had cells that might've turned abnormal in time. Your polyp had a high density of abnormal cells. It was noninvasive, caught very early, but it was cancer. Your chance of a recurrence is seventy percent. The only way to make sure that doesn't happen is to remove the colon."

In all of Howie's exhaustive research, including a phone call and email exchange with a researcher who'd worked side by side with Dr. Lynch himself, he hadn't heard or read this recommendation before.

"Why can't I just get screenings?" I asked.

"Colonoscopy is a useful tool, but it's not a guarantee. The doctor could miss something. Patients can get lazy about scheduling," he said. "I've seen it happen." He told the story of a patient of his who'd missed one colonoscopy and, wouldn't you just know, that was the year he'd bloomed a tumor.

I was a completely healthy woman. Cancer free, relatively young, a new vegetarian, could run eight miles. And yet a doctor who had yet to lay a hand on me was telling me to scoop out nearly every organ below the waist or I would get cancer and die. My mother's face turned white as bone. She didn't handle bad news well. I was worried about her. Howie stared at the guy, processing, thinking, thinking. I could practically hear his hard drive spinning.

Bow Tie said, "Compared to the minor inconvenience of a hysterectomy, having the colon removed is . . . why are you laughing?"

I said, " 'The minor inconvenience of a hysterectomy'? It's not like picking up the dry cleaning." Would he tell a man that cutting his nuts off was a minor inconvenience? Doubt it.

Doctors—except for Howie—often lack a sense of humor. Bow Tie said, "Ha. Ha. Hmm. I was explaining that colectomy would change your life, but over time you'd adjust. I have a patient, a college professor, who was in your situation and chose to have her colon removed. It's been a couple of years, and she can teach her classes, travel, play sports . . ."

"My husband had his colon removed twenty-five years ago," I said. "He's *still* adjusting." In his twenties, Steve suffered from colitis. When it became severe, his colon was cut out. His remaining tubing was rerouted and reconnected. He didn't have a bag, and his life was pretty normal. But every day he had some pain. Every day, he had to plan.

"I'm just informing you of Major Cancer Center's recommendations," said Bow Tie. "Some people choose to take the risk of annual screenings instead of surgery."

And then he left to go rock the world of the people in the next room. I tried to remember that he was not a bad person, even if his disaffected manner left a lot to be desired. He had to deliver wrenching news over and over all day long. What a job.

The Russian genetic counselor took over again. She said, "I know this is a lot to take in. This time last year, you were a healthy family, no sign of problems on the horizon. And now the picture has changed." Then she made her own set of recommendations—for about twenty thousand dollars' worth of additional tissue testing that was redundant or might be inconclusive, but that would further Major Cancer Center's research at the expense of my insurance company.

I said, "This is why there's a health care crisis in America."

I felt as if I'd spent the hour with a pair of used-car salesmen. Bow Tie pressuring me to buy surgeries. The counselor pressing me to buy tests. I wasn't convinced I needed any of it. What if I hadn't had insurance? Would they have been so determined to empty my pelvis?

Cynical? What of it? Even if the gene team's recommendations would save my life, I still felt badgered and bullied. I found it hard not to hate both of them.

A nurse took some blood. The counselor gave me a detailed list of the tests she wanted to run, what they'd cost, and a directory of the center's surgeons. Howie, Judy, and I left the center, dazed. We'd planned on having an early lunch.

None of us was hungry. They headed toward their car to drive back to New Jersey. I walked toward the subway and called Steve.

He was shocked by the news. "You can't get a colectomy," he said, "We'd have to fight each other for the bathroom."

"The last thing the counselor gave me was a list of on-site shrinks who specialized in patients with Lynch or the breast cancer gene," I said. "They've got it all. One-stop shopping. The Lowe's for cancer."

By the time I got home, I needed to make light of the situation. "Without any internal organs, I might finally have a waist," I said to Steve. "Your birthday's coming up. Maybe, as a gift, I'll put my womb in a jar. Brain cancer is on the Lynch hit list, too. I'm surprised they didn't recommend cutting off my head."

I felt bad about Steve's vasectomy. I'd be spayed shortly; he'd been neutered for nothing.

"That's ridiculous," he said.

I called Alison and told her what she'd missed. I recycled my jokes "cut off my head," "finally have a waist," etc. When our laughs stopped, melancholy set in. No reputable doctor would tell someone to have herself gutted unless he believed it was really necessary.

I called Dr. Guts (remember him? Mid-fifties, nice, Jewish?). He thought that annual screenings would be enough. I called a genetics researcher I'd consulted at Stanford University for her opinion. She said to be vigilant about scheduling. Disembowelment? No.

The decision not to do it could be the worst one I ever

made. Did I owe it to my children to have my colon removed, to do whatever I could to stay alive for them? Steve said, "If you do get colon cancer—like your grandmother, who lived to be, what, ninety?—you'll deal with it."

Back in the halcyon days before my first pathology report came in, I'd been confident I could face whatever reality might come. I'd been brave for Glenn, after all. I recalled moments during his illness and imagined switching places with him. It was me in the wheelchair, me in the chemo lounger, me in the hospital bed. Steve was pushing the chair, sitting nearby, cleaning up.

The visions were alarming, jarring, repellent. Why the strong reaction, apart from the obvious?

Steve wasn't the most organized person. Could he keep track of medications and appointments? Hardly loquacious, could he handle the incoming phone calls and updates? Not at all bureaucratically aggressive, would Steve demand answers from obtuse doctors, and do battle with my insurance company? Providing love and support were the easy parts of being a cancer spouse. The logistics, paperwork, and minutiae would try the strength of Xena. Steve wouldn't be able to disappear to Pete's or into a mood if I got sick.

The nugget of doubt lodged in my head and grew there, sort of like—oh, I dunno—*a tumor.* I didn't want to overdramatize any of this—*you are not sick,* I chided myself, *nothing has actually happened*—but that meeting at Major Cancer Center played havoc on my confidence in Steve. Thus far, in our marriage, I'd nursed him after he had a heart procedure, when he broke his arm, when he broke his toe. I was a big baby when I had a cold, but thus far, even after my 'oscopies, I'd been a low-maintenance patient. What would happen if I needed serious assistance? As a caretaker, Steve hadn't been tested.

I tried to ignore the nugget (you think I'd *learn*). But it wouldn't stop throbbing. Days went by, a week. The doubt grew and grew until I could no longer keep it in. I felt compelled to say something.

At 3:00 AM, naturally, aka the Bitching Hour.

I shook Steve awake, and said, "Look, are you going to get on the phone and challenge my insurance company over every bill they refuse to pay?"

Not fully awake, he said, "Whaaa?"

"You escape to Pete's when you're not even stressed out. If I got sick, would you move there? Set up a cot behind the bar?"

"I have no idea what you're talking about," he said.

"You haven't even Googled 'Lynch syndrome,'" I said. "Have you read any of the articles Howie sent?"

Awake now, Steve rubbed his eyes and turned to face me. He didn't look happy. "I have Googled 'Lynch,'" he said. "I talked to Dave [his childhood friend from Maine, an MD] about it, and I read the *JAMA* articles."

"Why didn't you say something, then?" I asked.

"Say what? 'Yup, looks bad'? I've been known to Google 'belly button lint.' Do you really think I don't care enough about your health to do a search?"

This was getting off track. "I need to know you're up for whatever might happen," I said. "If I'm too weak to get up and down the stairs, or in and out of the car, or to feed myself, or clean myself."

Now he looked hurt. I could see it in the dark. "Of course I'll do those things, and whatever else needs doing."

I flashed suddenly to last year, when Maggie and Lucy had stomach bugs. They didn't always get to the bathroom in time. While I comforted them, Steve did the wet work, the cleaning up. He carried Lucy up and down our three flights when her legs were in casts after her Achilles' tendon surgery. When Maggie had pneumonia, Steve took her to the doctor, twice, got her meds, monitored her recovery. He *had* been tested, and he'd excelled. Why had I blanked out on those times?

I said, "Why do you run away to the bar?"

"We spend more time together than any other couple we know," he said. "When you and the kids need me, I'm here. I go to Pete's when you *don't* need me."

"What if I need you all the time?"

"Then I'll be here, all the time," he said, starting to get angry. "You're not afraid I won't take care of you, Val. You're afraid of getting sick, of being out of control and helpless. You hate the idea of having to rely on someone else, even me. You trust me enough to adopt Maggie and Lucy; you trust me to take care of the kids if anything happened to you. But you don't trust me to take care of you if anything happened to you?"

I said, "That's a whole lot of 'you' sentences in a row." He was completely right, about all of it. My worries weren't about him. I was terrified about being needy. Showing weakness was my weakness. I guess I'd rather foist doubt on Steve, whom I loved and trusted implicitly, than admit to any vulnerability.

How often had I turned the tables on Steve in this way? He probably saw through it every time.

"What is I feel like a complete idiot right now?" I said

He mumbled. "Go to sleep."

And *that* was how to hate the man you loved, I thought. You underestimated him.

Eight

Why I Have No Friends, Part II

I turned forty-five in January. The middle of life, should I be so lucky.

"Do you want a party or a dinner?" Steve asked the week before.

"No party, no gifts. I'm not in the mood," I said honestly.

"You seem like you're in one, actually," he said.

Mood was the euphemism I used when he was depressed. My experience with the blues was practically nil. I tended to get mad, not sad. After Glenn died, I was advised by a dozen people to go on Prozac. Covering my bases, I went to a shrink to talk about it. After an hour, she said, "You're grieving, not depressed," and dismissed me. I'd seen the ravages of depression in some of my friends, who found relief via pills. I believed I was immune.

But as my birthday got closer, and on the day itself, despite receiving requisite calls and emails, I was down. An unforeseen complication, by opening myself up to loud negative emotions such as rage and jealousy, I had unwittingly let their quieter cousin slip in as well.

Steve's opera company's annual run at Carnegie Hall's City Center was under way, and he was busy rehearsing, performing, or practicing the horn. His mom and niece came down from Maine to watch him as Major General Stanley in *The Pirates of Penzance*. As hosts, we took the out-of-towners to dinner at an expensive Midtown restaurant. Later that night, Maggie and Lucy were both sick as dogs with food poisoning. The next day, I called the restaurant's manager to complain. He reluctantly agreed to reimburse us for the price of the offending dish only. The kids were ill for two days. Maggie lost a dangerous amount of weight. Meanwhile, I was in limbo about a couple of magazine things, waiting for either the approval on a pitch, a revise memo, or an overdue check. As soon as the City Center run was over, Steve left on a southern tour.

I was lonely, despairing, guilt-ridden about picking the restaurant that had made the kids sick, anxious about where my next assignment was coming from. A change in my pattern, instead of "switching off" the negative emotions, I sank into them. I felt exhausted, defeated, quick to cry—even more than usual, and not only while watching *The Biggest Loser*.

An entire day was lost to spirit-leaching Lynch syndrome chores, filling out forms at one hospital to arrange transfer of my tissue samples to the pathology department of another. I had my blood drawn, and had to drive miles into Brooklyn to a special FedEx branch that would ship "dangerous goods" overnight to the genetic research lab at Stanford University in California. The day of paperwork and blood work reminded me of the X-ray ferrying, insurance-form filling out, and other cancer chores I had done for Glenn, which brought up painful memories I'd buried for ten years. Writing provided no distraction. Workouts were hard to get through.

Depression had come, and I had no idea what to do. It seemed to like fatty, sugary snacks and long afternoon naps. Not that Maggie liked my cooking, but she didn't want takeout every night. "Snap out of it," she said—which I'd said, just as pointlessly, to Steve. Lucy said she was upset that she couldn't make me happy. I'd never put this kind of burden on my kids, and I felt terrible guilt, which made me sadder. I knew I was responsible for my own happiness, but I couldn't seem to manage it. Steve called a few times a day from Tennessee or Florida, wherever he was, but those truncated long-distance conversations only increased the sense of distance between us.

"Call a friend," he said.

Rebecca was out of town reporting an article. Daryl was on vacation. Nancy was starting her own business and barely had time to eat. I didn't want to bother anyone with my gloominess.

"You're my friend," I said to Steve over the in-and-out reception of the cell phone.

Lucy came home from school and announced, "I got a ninety-two on my geometry test!" It'd been a hard section for her; she was excited about her grade.

Maggie came home and said, "I got a part in the play!" Not a big part—a chorus girl in *Grease*—but the competition had been fierce. She was among the few freshman in the cast.

An overdue check arrived in the mail. I secured an assignment. Steve's tour ended and he was back at home, in our bed at night. Suddenly, as if it'd never been there, the depression was gone.

I knew it would have faded faster, though, if I'd had someone other than Steve to vent to. One or two trustworthy friends. The lack of confidantes had launched my career as a teenage hater. It was just plain SAD!!! that, all these years later, I was in the same sorry boat.

A (former) friend of mine wrote in a magazine article last year, "When a woman tells me that her husband is her best friend, what I hear is: I don't really have any friends." When I read that, I laughed out loud, thinking, "Guilty as charged!"

Hard not to hate the social-skilled women (and men) who were good at parties, had loads of friends and juggled them effortlessly. My envy of butterflies was rooted in the knowledge that I'd once been one. When I first moved to New York after college, I could walk into a roomful of strangers with a smile and walk out with ten phone numbers. Nowadays? I dreaded parties and hadn't made a new friend in years.

Friend-friend, I mean. Intimate. I had loads of work friends and friend*ly* human interaction. Meetings, lunches, school functions. I went to the gym a lot, and sometimes talked to people there. But I tended to keep a clear social calendar. My schedule always seemed full with deadlines, the kids, the house, Steve, our families. I had little time for my old friends, let alone for making new ones. Real friendship required more than posting a witty status update on Facebook. Attention must be paid. But the effort to make plans, which were usually rescheduled at least once, and to haul my lazy ass to a restaurant for lunch or the theater for a movie could sap my energy reserves.

During my twenties, I stayed home alone on a Saturday night *maybe* once, because I had the flu. When I wasn't at work, I was at play. My phone rang off the hook. In sprawling numbers, my friends and I roamed New York City, going to parties, concerts, restaurants, bars, and clubs. I accepted every invitation. I would have RSVP'd yes to the opening of a tin can. My job— entry-level magazine assistant—supplied ample perks (if a tiny salary) and kept me flush with passes to screenings, parties, clubs. I'd call whomever—even someone I'd met the night before—and we'd go out, meet more people, extend the burgeoning web of connections. Friends fell into categories. Wing women for bar crawling when in search of my next boyfriend. Guy friends to console me when my latest relationship ended. Perpetually single friends who were always available for chilling. The pals who offered a shoulder to cry on, a sofa to crash on, a booty call. Whatever my social need, I had a pal or two to meet it.

All those friendships, at the time, felt intense and deep. I believed they'd last forever. Hardly any did. I would get real close, real fast, with new people, and they'd disappear just as quickly. The office friend at my first job never called after I got fired. The female friend of a boyfriend dumped me a few days after he did. For months we'd spent every night hanging out, baring our souls. When I ran into her on the street a couple of years later, it was like we were complete strangers.

When a serious boyfriend entered the picture, friends got short shrift. Guy friends drifted away, and wing women flew the coop. At first Glenn and I were an out-and-about couple. He was in a band, and I invited all my pals to come hear him play at a club or bar. The band broke up and we traded the East Village scene for small dinner parties and double dates at West Village cafés. Glenn and I spent nearly all our time with other couples.

Where were they now? Did they all flee to the suburbs after 9/11? I lost touch with some after Glenn died. Some couples got divorced. Or they moved to another city. With a few, a fight or misunderstanding killed the friendship.

I was thirty when Maggie was born. Glenn and I were the first among our friends to reproduce. We swore that the baby wouldn't change our social lives—just one example of how clueless we were about the demands of parenthood. Glenn and I couldn't indulge in marathon dinner parties anymore. Or accept last-minute invites. Or drive a hundred miles to a concert. Rushing home to relieve the babysitter, we couldn't linger at post-work happy hours. Pals were annoyed ("I'm sorry Maggie has a cold, but this is the third time in a row you've canceled on me"), bored ("Yeah, you already mentioned that the baby rolled over. Whoopee."), or baffled ("I don't get it. You see Maggie every night. Why do you have to rush home to see her *again*?").

Some friends quietly slipped away. Others exploded with high drama. One very close friendship ended on the phone, when the friend accused me of cutting her off after Maggie was born. She was absolutely right. In this particular case, the friendship was too encompassing, she was too demanding. I used Maggie as an excuse to put some physical and emotional distance between us. She figured it out, called me on it. I admitted the truth, that I felt suffocated by her. As soon as I got the space I longed for, though, I felt a void.

I relied on professional friendships, the editors and writers I worked with, to fulfill my human interaction needs. Then Lucy was born, and the pressure of having two kids, working full time at *Mademoiselle,* and writing novels at night was too much. Glenn had a good job with health benefits. I went freelance. Professionally, I loved being my own woman. No marathon meetings in conference rooms, ten people debating the merits of a five-word caption. (Never thought I'd miss those.) For a while, I called my ex-colleagues to chat from my home office. It wasn't the same as flipping through magazines with our feet up on each other's desks. Strong work friendships grew feeble. Only a few survived.

Between thirty and thirty-five, my friendship losses were drastic. I certainly didn't mourn for the underminer who insulted me in public whenever she got the chance. Or the college pal who uncomfortably glommed on to my work friends. Or the insensitive woman who said, "I know how I'll get rich! I'll write some crappy chick-lit novel and sell it for a million dollars. How hard can it be?" For the most part, I was well rid of the friends I lost. Most of them were casual friends, expendable.

Casual, by the way, was the psychological term to describe one of four types of friendship:

1. Acquaintances. Most people had fifty to one hundred. The familiar faces on the street, at the gym or playground.

2. Casuals. Ten to fifty. A jogging partner, book club member, happy hour regular.
3. Close. Five to twenty. Trusted comrades you had a history with, cared about, and could say anything to.
4. Lifer. One to five. The person you can't imagine life without. A trustworthy pal to vent to, to rely on, a shield against anxiety and loneliness.

Famed British anthropologist Robin Dunbar once theorized that the maximum number of relationships any one person could maintain was 150, aka "Dunbar's number." Interestingly, that is close to the sum of the average friendship-type totals. Seventy-five acquaintances, 30 casuals, 15 close, and 3 lifers added up to 123. Throw in 27 family members to consider yourself Dunbared. Not everyone could maintain 150 relationships, though. Some people (ahem), on a good week, could handle maybe 10, including the dry cleaner and the Fresh Direct delivery guy.

Adult women who scrounged to rack up the casuals seemed like insecure teenagers to me. Overbooked butterflies in constant motion, maybe they worried that if they slowed down and took a hard look at themselves, they wouldn't like what they saw. Members of book clubs, coffee klatches, card games, play groups, and workout teams couldn't read a novel, change a diaper, or go on a diet without dragging someone else into it.

When Glenn got sick, we were impressed by the volume of acquaintances and casuals who offered wishes, prayers, and support, although we suspected that much of it was dutiful. One father from school made a friendly overture and asked if he could come over to spend some time with Glenn. Glenn agreed, thinking the dad, an overtly religious man, might have some wisdom to offer. The dad stayed for two hours. No wisdom. No advice. Just tedious, exhausting small talk. We later found out he used the visit to satisfy his church's community service requirement. Whenever I saw him around the neighborhood, I pulled a Williamsburg on him.

Some of my friends couldn't handle the gravity of Glenn's situation. They made perfunctory calls, but mainly they avoided us. If an offer of support sounded tinny and false, I soured on the person and the friendship. It was as if I'd grown a new pair of ears that were super sensitive to insincerity. By exchanging only a few syllables with someone, I knew if she was genuine and trustworthy or specious and motivated by guilt or macabre inquisitiveness.

A few days after Glenn's diagnosis, an old friend, Karen, called and said, "I was hurt that I had to hear about Glenn from someone else. You should have told me!"

I'd had the time, courage, and desire to call only a few people. "Sorry about that," I said.

"What did the doctor say?" she asked.

"That Glenn has cancer," I replied.

"But what's the prognosis? How many years? Will he have surgery? What about chemo?"

My skin started to creep. "I've got to go," I said. "I'll call you."

Her prodding for medical details seemed voyeuristic, grotesque. The whole conversation made me queasy. I didn't call her with the promised updates, partly due to the bad vibes, but mainly because I had bigger concerns than satisfying her curiosity.

Years later, we met for a catching-up coffee. Karen said she was upset at Glenn's funeral, but not because she was saying goodbye to a thirty-four-year-old man who died way too soon.

"I made a big effort to get there," she said, "and then you barely spoke to me. I saw you hug _____, and you don't even like her!"

I said, "I was a bit distracted that day. Burying my husband. Taking care of Maggie and Lucy, who'd just lost their father."

"Of course," she said. "I know you were busy. But you hurt my feelings."

Karen and I haven't spoken since that coffee. Never again would be too soon.

A couple of friendships survived Glenn's death but not my marriage to Steve. One friend said, "Maggie and Lucy will never love Steve like they loved Glenn. They'll resent you for marrying someone else." That was our last dinner together.

My longtime friend Jake was a rock during my widow year. He came over whenever I called. He dragged me out of the house, too. When I cleaned out Glenn's closet, Jake loaded the fifteen huge bags into his truck and took them to the Salvation Army. Then I started seeing Steve, whom Jake couldn't relate to. Around the same time, he started dating his future wife, who seemed cold to me. Not long after his wedding—I was among the few he asked to prepare a toast—our friendship faded. I hadn't spoken to him in years. Even more incredibly, I didn't miss him.

When a friendship ended and you didn't mourn the loss, "The essential trust was missing, no matter how much you thought otherwise," said Rebecca, one of my lifers. That rang true about Karen, she of the "hurt feelings." But Jake? We had essential trust. But as I'd come to realize, although I considered him one of my best buds, a keeper, he probably thought of me differently. He'd stayed in my life after Maggie and Lucy were born. But when his children arrived and he had to start lopping peripherals off his list, I failed to make the cut.

And Steve? Did he bring friends to the table? I liked his pals—musicians, singers, dancers, and actors. But I hadn't bonded intimately with any of them. Steve was the oldest of seven siblings. I adored his three sisters, but they lived in Maine, 450 miles away. We had great fun when we got together twice a year, but we weren't close.

Which brought me to where I was now, at forty-five, counting my lifers on one hand.

I could try to make new friends, but that would be challenging. Paula, my friend and editor at *Self,* told me recently, "When I first met you, you scared the crap out of me." I guess I didn't make the warmest first impression.

Tomas, a lifer from college, said, "Easy or not, you have to try. Making new friends is like working a muscle. If you don't exercise it, it'll atrophy. You might lose the ability entirely."

Attracting people when I was a boy-crazy, up-for-anything twenty-three-year-old had been a piece of cake. But now that I was a mortgage-holding stressed-out working mother (but funny?), who would want to take me on? I would have crossed the street to get away from myself.

In all honesty, some women did make overtures. "When are we going to get that drink?" they said, or "You should come to our country house for a weekend." When a woman asked me to dinner, I felt instantly suspicious, as if she wanted something from me, even thought I knew she was just being, er, *friendly*. The idea of nurturing casuals into close friends felt like another part-time job. When I had plans, I felt a sense of dread and had to psyche myself up to get out the door. But then I'd have a great time and wonder why I didn't go out more often. When opportunity came again, however, I'd wave at it as it passed by.

I loved cozy nights at home with Steve, the kids, the cats, my books, Netflix, and Tivo. For all my agoraphobic contentment, though, I felt inferior to socially active women. I watched them in pairs and trios around the neighborhood, going to yoga classes, double-dating, drinking gallons of coffee in cafés.

Authentic emotions check: I thought I should be socially adept. I was socially inept.

Rebecca and I talked about this a lot. "Even if the moms *had* invited me to get coffee after drop-off," she said one day when she learned that a group of them kept a biweekly date, "I wouldn't want to go. I'd come up with an excuse. And if I did go, I'd probably hate it." But not getting invited? Instant flashback to junior high.

"How do you do it?" I asked Laura, my popular friend.

"Do what?"

"Have so many friends."

"What friends? I've got five friends," she said.

"What about all those parties and dinners? You're always out, doing things, seeing people, throwing barbecues," I said.

"If you were invited to a party and you recognized everyone there, would you classify them as 'friends' or just as 'people you know'?" she said.

"But I'm never invited to parties," I said. "Except yours."

"I get asked out because people want me to entertain

them," she said. "I don't feel a deep connection with them. But I like the attention."

Laura was entertaining. Put a few glasses of wine in her and it was comedy night at the Improv. She thrived on the attention and approval of others. When people laughed at her jokes, or told her she looked beautiful (boy, did she), Laura would grow inches before my eyes.

I liked attention, too. Critical attention for my books. In social situations, I shrank from the spotlight like a vampire at dawn. My usual party position was in the corner with Steve and/or one other person, talking, watching, making comments. If anything, I craved more alone time. All of my hobbies were solitary. Gardening, reading, cooking, jogging while listening to the iPod. I relied on Steve and the kids for necessary companionship.

Watching an episode about the importance of friendship of *This Emotional Life* on PBS, I was pleased to see a segment with Laura Carstensen, PhD, professor of psychology and director of the Stanford Center on Longevity, whom I'd interviewed once for a magazine article.

I called her the next day to ask about my too-limited social scope. "We live in a 'the more, the better' culture," she said. "If a little bit of something is good, then a lot of it must be better. That's not necessarily true of friends. Having a few close, deep friendships is better than having a large number of casual ones. Smaller networks predict positively for mental health. Large networks? Not so much," she said. "It's better to have a small group of close friends you adore than fifty peripherals."

How small a group? There was, actually, a minimal friend requirement. "Three is the lowest you ever want to go," said

Carstensen. "You need at least three people who are close and central to your life. Three people who will drop anything for you, whom you would drop anything for, who are deep and almost like family. Dip below three and you won't have adequate emotional support, you'll be vulnerable to loneliness, isolation, anxiety, and you could fall into depression." This number could include family members, but "there is evidence that voluntary networks—people you choose to be your 'family' versus the family you were born into—might be better for your mental health," said Carstensen. "For one thing, a voluntary family doesn't include Uncle Ned who gets drunk every Christmas."

Three. It seemed so few. It was, actually, "a few." The problem with having less than a handful of friends: one day, you could wind up empty-handed. People changed. Circumstances changed. Anything could happen, and probably would— relocation, philosophic or political shifts, sudden fortune, sudden misfortune, death. It was entirely possible that I could look up from my computer years from now to find I didn't have any friends left. That my handful had slipped through my fingers.

In late January we adopted a kitten, a fluffy white charmer named Bunny. According to her veterinary records, she was the cutest kitten ever to have lived. She was our fourth. Four cats was a lot, but still a dozen short of total bat-shit crazy.

Daryl came by to meet Bunny. "How was your birthday?" she asked.

The words, "Fine. Good," were on my lips. But I swallowed the lie and said, "Horrible, actually. I was depressed."

"Why didn't you call me?" she asked.

"You were out of town."

"A neat little invention you might have heard of," she said. "The cell phone? It works, even in Boston."

"It's okay," I said, backpedaling. I dreaded a sticky "moment," like if she put her arms around me, let me cry on her shoulder, or sang a bar of the treacly "That's What Friends Are For."

Sensing my discomfort, Daryl said, "Well, you should have called."

We turned our attention back to Bunny, who was letting us rub her belly. "Now I have almost as many cats as I have friends," I said.

"Okay, that's it," Daryl said. "Speaking on behalf of all the friends you don't have," she said, "we're sick of hearing you say that."

"When I say, 'I have no friends' . . ."

"Which you do *way* too often," she said.

"I know I have friends," I said. "The few, the filth . . ."

"When am I supposed to take you seriously?" she asked. "How depressed *were* you on your birthday? And you didn't call anyone—not even Rebecca?"

I felt desperately squirmy now—which, habitually, would have had me kicking into "glossing over" mode or putting on a poker face. "And say what?" I asked, " 'Hello, it's me. I'm, heavy sigh, blue today?' "

"I'm sure you can do better than that," she said.

"And you'd really want me to prove it?"

"As uncomfortable as it makes you, that is what friends are for," she said. "You really can say anything to me. I loved your 'I'm jealous' period. That was fun."

I nodded, considered. "Okay, you asked for it. Remember when I had all of those scans back in May?" I asked.

"Yeah?"

"There've been some developments," I said. "Some things I haven't told you."

The obvious becomes glaring only when a light shines upon it. It seemed obvious to us now that something was amiss on my dad's side of the family. But until the family tree with all those blackened squares and circles was printed out, no one had noticed.

Another entry in the obvious-but-missed category: I knew I was good at hiding pain from my enemies, but somehow, without realizing or understanding the danger, I'd gotten in the habit of hiding pain from my friends as well. I tended to gloss over difficult emotions without appreciating that love and reliance could be included in that category. I thought I'd been protecting my friends from my gloom and worries. But I'd only been protecting myself from admitting I had those worries, and from the possibility of rejection. A foolish fear. My lifers—all of them twenty-year friendships or longer— had been through the ringer with me, and had stuck by me no matter what. I should have trusted them.

Daryl was shocked I hadn't told her about the horrible day at Major Cancer Center, what Bow Tie had advised me to do, and the hysterectomy to come. It had been particularly non-sensical to hold out on Daryl: her sister was a gynecological oncologist.

The bough broken, I started making calls, went out to dinners, and told my lifers what was going on and what was coming up. I opened my arms to bathetic hugs and my ears to "I'm there for you," "How can I help?" My super-sensitive hearing detected not a whit of insincerity.

I heard myself admitting, out loud, "Yes, thank you, I will need help. Babysitting, hospital visits, dinners. I accept." I even (gasp) cried a little.

Sappy was only nauseating in overly sentimental novels. In real life, expressing your appreciation and love for friends was quite palatable, in small doses. It might be a while yet before I could group-hug without smirking, though.

Nine

·················

Why Pot Should Be Legal

I *swear* I was in a good mood. It was a clear, crisp day. Lucy and I were out and about, shopping in the neighborhood. We walked by a Subway restaurant. Lucy said she was hungry. We entered the place—it was completely empty—and went up to the counter. The only worker behind it ignored us while she restocked the food containers—for, like, ten minutes.

Finally, she asked for our order. "Six-inch tuna on untoasted wheat, just tuna, no cheese, no veggies," I said, knowing how Lucy liked hers.

Moving as if through cement, the sandwich maker (sandista?) got to it. "Lettuce?" she asked.

"Just tuna, nothing else, thanks," I repeated.

"Tomato?"

"Just tuna." Was she deaf?

"Cheese?" asked the sandista.

"Just *tuna,*" I snapped. "*Just tuna, just tuna, just tuna.*"

"Calm down, lady," she replied, which, quite understandably, made me want to tear her face off.

By the time we paid and left, my brain had reached a rapid boil, reducing to a simmer on the walk home. Lucy told Steve the story. "Mom had a tuna meltdown," she said, which was pretty funny. I laughed, but Steve was not amused.

He said to Lucy, "The girl at Subway was just doing her job. Not well, but it's not such a great job. Mom shouldn't have snapped at her."

I driveled out a defense—"No matter what your job is, Lucy, you should do it to the best of your ability"—but I felt the guilt.

Any reasonable person would have been annoyed by the sandista. Exactly whom was she calling "lady," anyway? But my onrush of antipathy for a stranger in a sandwich shop might have been a bit over the top. In front of my kid! Steve was right. I should have controlled myself.

We've all been there. Perhaps you actually were there, the very next day, on an endless line at Banana Republic, a line that snaked miles back into menswear, when some selfish, clueless *idiot* brought in two shopping bags of returns on a sales day. The cashier giggled each time her register beeped in error every three seconds. Apparently, her incompetence was freaking *hilarious*. The peripatetic manager appeared to insert a magic key into the register to make it stop beeping, only to wander off, perhaps into the storeroom to snort heroin. When the register complained again, the people on line had to wait for the manager to rematerialize with the key. Why didn't he stand by to help the cashier, or simply leave the key in the machine?

Why, for the love of *Christ,* didn't he open *another* register, so the irate customers could purchase our overpriced *crap* made in China and get out of there?

During the interminable wait, I kept myself busy blasting gusts of fury from my nostrils like a bull and fantasizing about the cashier's head bursting into flames. Some of the women waited patiently—freaks!—as if they had all day to placidly compose sonatas in their heads. One woman yelled into her cell to some poor slob (assistant? husband?) about the disgrace of her three-year-old's failure to earn a spot in a preschool program for gifted thumb-suckers.

It was hard not to hate her. As well as the cashier, the manager, the idiot with the mountain of returns, the calm freaks who made me feel like a rage-aholic.

Seeking consolation, I made eye contact with the clearly annoyed woman on line ahead of me. She flashed a sympathetic smile, and then her face froze. She instinctively stepped back. Odd. Then I caught my reflection in a wall mirror. My face was red, my hair frizzed from aggressive raking, my mouth a tight zag, eyes wild and glowing with barely suppressed rage. I looked like the crazy cat lady on *The Simpsons.* I felt an urge to step away—from myself.

Transformation to Val Black complete.

I flashed back to a night over the summer when I had the same unhinged look, out on my deck after midnight, in my bathrobe, with snarled sleep hair, crazed eyes, and a pitchfork, to rail at my college-age next-door neighbor, Eric. He'd been partying with his friends on the adjacent deck all night. Loudly. Practically right under my bedroom window. Drinking their damn *beer*. Smoking their damn *pot*. Laughing at their damn *jokes*.

Hours earlier I had been out on the deck in a much different state of mind, watering my container garden in a tank top and shorts, my hair in a pony tail. I thought I looked sort of cute, in a slightly chubby middle-aged way (be nice), holding a hose, barefoot among the flowers and plants as the sun set. Eric's party was just getting started, half a dozen nineteen-year-old boys were congregating ten feet from where I watered. Although Eric's mother (the famous shrink who'd called my goal of writing a bestseller "shallow") usually upheld the "invisible wall" between our two decks, Eric always said hello, was chatty, friendly, and polite.

So he waved. His friends followed his example. I reciprocated, smiling, and went about my business, wondering whether any of those college boys considered me a MILF.

If they had—not saying they did—my MILF status was knocked down by my second appearance on the deck, at 1:00 AM, raving, ranting, a haggy crone with a gaping maw screaming at the youngsters to stop making such a racket.

I'd held back as long as I could. Every five minutes for an hour, I'd said to Steve, "Don't they realize people are trying to sleep?"

Steve, who could sleep through a terrorist attack, grumbled, "Incredible as it might seem, Eric and his friends aren't thinking about you and your insomnia right now."

"I'm doing it," I said finally, and threw back the covers, stormed outside, and demanded that they shut up or go inside. Like the party police. Like I'd never been nineteen or had a beer and a smoke. When I came back inside and got into bed, I was more riled up than ever. No *way* could I fall asleep now that I'd embarrassed myself—and Eric, which I hadn't thought about until afterward.

If I'd been patient, waited for the party to wind down, I might have gotten some sleep. By impatiently breaking it up—they did go inside—I barely closed my eyes, and I spent most of the night thinking how ghastly I must have seemed to those kids.

I wondered how New York City folk hero John Clifford, aka the Etiquette Vigilante of the Long Island Rail Road, would have handled that situation, or the one at Banana Republic, or the Subway sandista. Clifford had been ticketed eight times for defending his right to common freaking courtesy. After a woman spilled some of her beverage on him and didn't apologize, he took her cup and emptied it over her head. He asked a loud cell phone talker, repeatedly and nicely, to lower her voice, and then cursed and went to slap her when she refused. Most famously, he allegedly threw an egg salad sandwich at another loud cell phone talker.

Erratic? Dangerous? Unhinged? Violence was never the answer. But according to an unofficial public opinion poll (me and my friend Rebecca), Clifford hadn't gone far enough. An ex-cop, Clifford was braver than the ordinary citizen. When I felt the urge to throw a sandwich at a loud cell phone talker, gum-snapping cashier, or giant-umbrella carrier, I usually swallowed the complaint and vented later to poor Steve.

Speaking up in New York could get you killed or put in the hospital. Movie theater shushers had been knifed. At a Ditmas Park, Brooklyn, bodega, a customer couldn't hear the cashier because of a loud cell phone talker on line behind her. She asked the talker to lower her voice, then paid for her goods and left the store. The talker followed her out, beat her with her stiletto heel, threw scalding hot coffee in her face, and bit her before police arrived and arrested the maniac for assault.

Usually, obnoxious cell-talker confrontations don't come to blows, just more loudness, as in the case of the opera singer who was asked to turn off her phone or leave a Lincoln Center restaurant. Diva-like, she refused, and proceeded to unleash an aria of invective (chest voice), before she was escorted away by cops. She later apologized to the restaurant owners.

Fighting back against inconsiderate dolts can be self-defeating, especially if you get brained with a stiletto. This was true, even for John Clifford, a lawyer, who'd lost days and weeks of his life in court defending his actions.

An alternative to raining egg salad sandwiches, howling at college kids at 1:00 AM? Be serene. Without a continuous intravenous THC drip, however, serenity seemed unlikely, given my rage-aholic nature. But surely I could get a few steps closer. Other people weren't epically deranged in traffic. At some point in their emotional development, they'd taught themselves how to calm the fuck down. Were long lines and rude people really so awful? Parents' night wasn't the gulag. Banana Republic and Duane Reade were not outposts of Guantánamo Bay.

Any minor inconvenience (say, a hysterectomy) overwhelmed my patience. Speaking of hysteria, my hair-trigger impatience was not related to that time of the frigging month. I got irritable at *every* time of the month, although my symptoms did spike pre-flow. Having surgery would surely cure me of that.

Seeing the bright side!
Emotions evolving at blinding speed.

Patience is a virtue. Is impatience, therefore, a sin? Or is it just a really bad habit in desperate need of breaking? Certainly, fretting furiously in place didn't make me a better person. And it wasn't a sign of superior health or intelligence. The opposite, in fact. Some studies:

- In 2007, researchers at the University of Bonn gave IQ tests to 1,000 Germans, followed by a test of their patience. "Individuals with higher cognitive ability were significantly more patient," quoted the paper.
- In 2008, researchers at Northwestern University gave 550 subjects two choices: a small-now versus larger-later check. The impatient subjects who grabbed the small-now checks took longer to cash them. Conclusion: Impatient subjects were, paradoxically, procrastinators.
- In 2004, researchers at the University of Munich and the University of Michigan–Dearborn drew a plausible link between impatience and (dear God, no) obesity, theorizing that Americans, in particular, would rather eat cake *right now* than wait (patiently) for weight loss to come later.
- Most alarmingly, a 2003 study of 3,000 18-to-30-year-olds found that impatient people "in young adulthood had a higher risk of developing hypertension

when examined fifteen years later," said the author, Lijing L. Yan, PhD.

Quite a snapshot. Impatient people were fat, stupid procrastinators with dangerously high blood pressure.

Besides being a bad role model and terrifying innocent bystanders, I was horrified that my impatience might lead to dangerous hypertension (heart disease: that was all I needed). The obesity threat? I shuddered. My impatience was clearly affecting the quality of my life and skyrocketing my stress, which I was supposed to be cutting back on.

I might need a personality transplant to do so. According to a test at Psychologytoday.com, I was an A student—as in a type A personality (actually, I fell between A and B; I was an A-). Of the test's nine subcategories (including drive, competitiveness, hostility, and perfectionism), my lowest mark was for "tough-mindedness"—a 21 out of 100—making me empathetic, open-minded, a big softie, basically, when it came to other people. My empathy score explained why I never got angry if kept waiting by a friend. On the other hand, when I was kept waiting in a doctor's office or by the GE repairman, I bubbled in a froth of apoplexy.

My highest mark on the type A test—76 out of 100—was for "time urgency," defined as "the state of being hurried and under pressure, as well as inclined to be impatient." Extreme time urgency impatience (TUI) was also known as Hurry Up syndrome, or, in my case, Hurry the Hell Up syndrome.

More Googling brought me to this astonishing checklist, originally created by the legendary shrink Meyer Friedman:

1. Does having to wait upset you? (Er, see previous paragraphs.)
2. Would you describe yourself as a fast eater? (The first to finish every meal.)
3. Are you still stressed at the end of the workday? (Does the workday end?)
4. Do you often feel under pressure? (Since I *am* under pressure a lot, yeah.)
5. Does your mind drift when you have a conversation with your significant other? (Only when he talks about Wagner operas and Vincent Price movies.)
6. In traffic, do you get annoyed and curse at other drivers? (Is *douchebag* a curse word?)
7. During meals, do you open a book or newspaper? (During toilet time, too.)
8. Do long lines at stores and late package arrivals bother you? (If *bother* means foaming at the mouth, then, yes.)

"I think I have TUI," I told Steve.

"Drink cranberry juice," he said.

If only TUI were that easy to treat. Had I ever not felt intense pressure? I was too impatient to search my memory to find out. Experts believe that personality traits such as optimism and extroversion are largely genetic and set in stone at birth. But impatience is not a trait. It is, per shrinks, a behavior. Any behavior can be modified.

But how? Re: my jealousy about Yvonne's *New York Times* bestseller, for example, and annoyance about the Biggest Bitch of All, merely acknowledging the hate took the edge off of it. *I am* as impatient as a tick. *I thought I should be* as serene as a Zen monk. Quite a gap.

While jogging to reduce stress one Sunday morning, I ran by a building I'd never noticed before, less than a mile from my apartment. The two-story edifice had a red brick facade, and probably dated back to the nineteenth century. The arched double doors were wide open. People in comfortable clothes were filing inside. Bells were plinking, incense burning. I asked a woman in a gray robe what was going on, and she said, "Sunday meditation is about to begin." I looked at the carved stone plaque above the doors. It read: "Zen Center of New York."

Mary T. Browne would probably ask, "Why did you decide to go for a run that early on a Sunday, take a different route than usual, and look up at that particular moment?" Since reading *Zen and the Art of Motorcycle Maintenance* at fifteen, I'd always equated that bent of Buddhism with supreme go-with-the-flow powers. Was it a coincidence that I'd jogged here with impatience on my mind? I'd been down that block a hundred times—it was on the way to Target—and hadn't noticed the Zen Center before. Not consciously anyway. But subconsciously? Apparently so.

Sweaty and red from jogging, I went in. A man in a gray robe said, "Please remove your shoes and find a mat."

Did he mean my disgusting running sneakers? "Er, my feet might . . . distract people," I said.

"I'll ask you to remove your shoes," he said, smiling.

Bombs away, I thought. "How long is the meditation?" I asked.

"Until noon." It was nine o'clock.

I stopped untying. *"Three hours?"* The one time I'd tried meditation in earnest I lasted about three minutes. Plus, religious services—religious anything—made me uncomfortable and suspicious. An ethnic Jew, I was secular, non-practicing. To be a temple member, I'd have to, one, pay thousands of dollars a year, and, two, join the club, which, in case you've been napping between sentences, was the kind of thing that made me break out in a grenade-shaped rash.

Bells bonged rapidly. The service was about to begin. I was swept along with the other observers, and found a mat inside the temple.

Nice room. Columns, big windows. An altar with a carving of Buddha and a box of incense burning like a mini brush fire. The place was packed with people, all ages, races, apparent classes, standing in front of black cushioned mats.

We were handed liturgy books, and the people around me started chanting, to the beat of a drum, a prayer about the wisdom of emptiness (made me hungry), releasing of desire (made me horny), and the pursuit of calm (made me sleepy). The woman to my right moved a step away from me. She probably would've liked to chant, "e-ven-the-in-cense-can-not-help-de-li-ver-me-from-the-stench-of-foot-o-dor-or-or."

Page after page we chanted. In English. In . . . Buddhist. Some prayers called the practice of Zen "the only way," phraseology that I'd heard in synagogues, churches, temples—the "my path beats yours" message that so turned me off to organized religion.

Newcomers were led up a wood-paneled stairway for beginning instruction on how to sit and breathe. I thought I already knew how to do those things, but I was mistaken. One newcomer rummaged in her purse, finding her water bottle, stuffing her phone inside, zipping and unzipping, about five full minutes after the twenty other beginners had settled down and were ready to begin. She seemed oblivious to the fact that forty eyes were on her, annoyed, waiting for her to stop fussing. She was exactly the kind of oblivious selfish person who sparked my twitchy impatience. Like the mother on Parents' Night at school who asks the teacher a long-winded question that pertains to her child only. Or a gym-goer who stays on the treadmill even though his thirty-minute time limit is up and five people are waiting for the machine. My blood started to roil over the purse rummager.

Where was an egg salad sandwich when I needed it?

The Zen instructor, a mid-thirties white woman, spoke in a soft, flat, breathy monotone. "I'll ask you to stop that," she said. "You, the woman with the water bottle and the cell phone. Yes, I'll ask you to stop that. Stop zipping and unzipping. Yes, now. Thank you."

It was hard not to *love her*. A direct, soothing request. "I'll ask you to" would be my new mantra. The Zen approach to dealing with infuriating, inconsiderate jerk-offs worked. The rummager seemed chastised. This was better than screaming, "Douchebag!" or leaking toxic "shushes."

After a brief instruction, the beginners rejoined the gray-robed flock. For the next two hours, I sat in a half-lotus. My leg fell asleep. I counted my breaths. The sensei led a Q-and-A session to address the particular challenge of being Buddhist in the New York culture saturated with ambition, competition, and wealth.

A young woman took the microphone and said, "Well, like, it's this thing I have in my life. From when I was, like, really young. My whole life, I've had this . . . it's this thing, that, like, is hard to explain. I have, like, a lot of, you know, all this pressure in my life. And I really, really want to, like, be successful, you know?"

The first step on her path to enlightenment should be learning how to *speak*. I started counting her "likes" and "you knows" and "in my lifes" as well as my breaths—and the minutes until I could leave.

The sensei, at the front of the room, didn't nod her along or make the winding hand gesture that signified, "For the love of *Christ, get on* with it." Maggie, when she made this gesture, sometimes accompanied it by saying, "Point?"

The sensei's advice, when it finally came, whistled between my ears. But I was in rapt amazement just looking at his face. He listened to each person's complaint in turn, some highly personal and totally irrelevant to the subject he'd introduced earlier. Not sure if this was a trait of Zen Buddhists, but every eager, earnest sharer who took the mike spoke with the clarity, diction, and articulation of a six-year-old with ADD. The sensei's answers and advice didn't necessarily resonate with me. But his astonishing patience with these blabbermouths? Heroic.

When the service ended, I put on my sneakers—they

hadn't, as I feared, crawled away without me—and jogged home. Doubted I'd return for more chanting, sitting, and breathing. But I did call the Zen Center the next day and got the sensei who'd so impressed me—one Geoffrey Shugen Arnold—on the phone.

"What's the dharma on patience?" I asked. "Or how can I learn not to tear my hair out?"

"Patience is a spiritual practice," said the sensei. "Patience is often misunderstood as waiting, being passive. But it's not passive at all. In our tradition, things have their own time, from cooking a meal to raising a child."

"It's natural to have reasonable expectations," I said.

"You can get in a car with a sense of how long a trip should take," he said. "But you're not in control of it. If your expectation is challenged—by traffic or roadwork—you're in conflict. Our inner sense tells us that something should be happening but isn't. We feel like that's wrong. But what's actually happening *is* what's happening. We want traffic to change or we'll feel distressed. But what really has to change is our reaction to traffic."

"I will never, *ever* learn to like traffic," I said.

"It's a matter of accepting your circumstances," he said, "and working within that context. Can you take a different route? If you're stuck, you can be actively engaged in the understanding that you can't control the world. We can work within it, not in opposition to it. It's not easy. Patience takes practice. Patience *is* a practice. Cultivate it with the awareness that every moment is when life is occurring, and live completely in the present moment in peace, even if it's in traffic."

. . .

I was eager to put the sensei's dharma to the test, to actively practice patience. Weirdly, for a couple of weeks, lines at stores zipped. Packages and checks arrived on time. People kept their mouths shut during movies. Trains and traffic ran smoothly. I drove to my sister's house on a Friday evening. Astonishingly, I didn't dip below forty-five miles per hour on the Long Island Expressway, a notorious traffic hazard. And no one cut me off! I started to feel impatient about not getting to be impatient.

Finally, opportunity knocked. Or, I should say, opportunity bludgeoned.

A travel day. Steve, Maggie, Lucy, and I woke up at 5:00 AM to fly home from a too-short Presidents' Day weekend vakay. At the airport, we learned that our seat reservations had mysteriously been deleted, and we had to take four middle seats rows apart. We boarded, but the plane sat on the tarmac for an hour, putting us at risk for missing our connecting flight. Once we got to the hub airport in Miami, we waited on endless lines at Customs and Immigration. We ran with our luggage to our connecting gate, only to find that the second flight had also been delayed, and our seat reservations were messed up again. We waited at that gate—now starving and tired (I refused to eat the swimming-in-grease airport fast food)—for an hour and a half. When we finally arrived at Kennedy Airport in Queens, we waited for thirty minutes on the taxi line. The traffic on the ride home to Brooklyn was horrendous. The driver stopped short every ten feet. Maggie, whose Dramamine had worn off hours ago, puked. I'd been on the verge of getting my period for days, and then I did, in the taxi, in my new white jeans.

Even while it was happening, I marveled at the confluence of out-of-my-control impatience provocateurs. Fatigue, hunger, inept service people, computer snafus, weather delays, PMS, a sick kid, as well as old favorites: long lines and traffic.

It was the perfect storm of impatience. Incredibly, I didn't drown, although I floundered for most of it. I tried distraction by reading a thriller by Lee Child. Didn't work. Every paragraph, I'd look up from my book to see that the line I was in hadn't moved an inch or that our flight was still delayed.

I tried to manage my expectations. Instead of thinking, "We should board the plane now," I thought, "We probably won't board for another five hours." And then, "We'll probably be stuck at this smelly gate for another ten hours. I'll be trapped here with screaming babies, the guy in the chair next to me snoring, the girls whining, Steve wandering off, for the rest of my entire fucking life." Not helping.

As the sensei advised, I tried to work within the context and not in opposition to it. I'd actively engage in understanding that I was living only this actual moment, in this rotten situation that I couldn't control—oh, yeah, and to be at peace. As I sat (not in a lotus) in my plastic seat at the gate, I breathed and concentrated furiously on accepting the circumstances.

Steve reappeared, smelling like beer, and said, "You look like you swallowed a cactus. What are you doing?"

"I'm practicing patience," I said, "by living in the $%&$# moment."

"Way to go, Grasshopper."

I felt myself darkening into Val Black, and feared that an

airline official might judge me dangerously unfit for travel. I imagined the scenario: walking onto the airplane—my cheeks bright red, hair frizzed, eyes wild and frantic—getting to my row, growling at some grandma in the window seat, "Buckle up, it's going to be a bumpy flight." Her screaming. Me being escorted off the plane, my husband cringing a few rows back, my daughters disavowing me, saying, "Mother? I don't even know her."

Made me laugh, immediately relaxing me. My blood pressure returned to normal. I started searching the crowd for other women at our gate on the verge of sinking into impatience-related insanity. I enlisted my kids to join me in the game of "Where's Wacko?" Next thing I knew, we were called to board the plane.

Meditation, accepting circumstances, and managing expectations were great ways to rein in impatience—for other people. But finding something to laugh about was my version, my practice of Zen. A-lit-tle-hu-mor-went-a-ve-ry-ve-ry-long-way. It got me all the way from Miami to New York. If I could remember to use it regularly, a little humor might get me through the rest of a healthy and happy life, which, unlike lines and traffic, I was in no hurry to see the end of.

Ten

. . . .

The Enemies List

In Nancy Mitford's classic novels *Love in a Cold Climate* and *The Pursuit of Love,* the character Uncle Matthew, a truculent bastard based on Mitford's own father, Lord Redesdale, took devilish pleasure in writing his enemies' names on little pieces of paper and then putting them in a particular drawer in his desk. Uncle Matthew believed—magically, his *secret*—that putting their names in a drawer sealed his enemies' doom. That soon after they'd suffer some horrible, unspeakable comeuppance, and he would rejoice in the knowledge that he alone had caused it.

Unlike Uncle Matthew, I didn't put names in a drawer. Please! The idea was ridiculous! If some chronically overdressed mother from the neighborhood looked snidely at my workout ensemble and said, "Don't you look *comfortable,*" I wouldn't rush home, head full of steam, grab a pen, scribble her name on a piece of paper, and put it in the drawer of reckoning.

I could imagine, however, how satisfying it might feel to

do so, albeit, in a pathologically petty way. It'd be one small (really small) act of attempting to rectify the insults and injustices of daily life. When I happened to witness this same woman accidentally spill the contents of her purse on the street a few days later, her lipstick in the gutter was a case of coincidental bad luck.

Or was it?

Okay, okay, I'll admit, I did put some names in a drawer, the top drawer of my home office desk. At this very moment I was sitting at the very desk where, as Daryl said, "The magic happens."

The black magic.

Sometimes the boomerang of fate hit fast and hard upon the people who'd wronged me. The new editor at *Mademoiselle* decided to kill my long-running advice column because, as she saw it, my "voice" wasn't a good fit for the magazine. My voice had been spot-on there for ten years—but, whatever. It was her magazine now. She could fire whomever she wanted. And I could retaliate. I showed this woman no mercy. Scribbled her name on a piece of paper, inserted it into the drawer. Three months later, *Mademoiselle* was no more, put out of business. The editor who canned me? She was blamed for bringing down the legendary magazine. Her reputation never fully recovered.

Eerily, when I looked in my drawer a week later, I noticed that the piece of paper with her name on it was singed, blackened around the edges, as if it'd been burned.

Had you going there for a second, didn't I?

Sometimes the boomerang missed the target. The oncologist who treated Glenn, I read recently, was given an award.

What would the selection committee members think if they knew their recipient stopped returning my calls when the experimental drug Glenn was taking failed and he was kicked off the trial? When I finally did get the doctor on the phone— only after I threw an absolute fit to his receptionist and threatened to write an exposé on him in the *New York Times* (as if)—he explained his disappearance by saying, "There's nothing I can do for him at this point."

That doctor's was the first name I wrote on a piece of paper and put in a drawer. Not the last.

As a person of taste, I preferred my revenge cold and my grudges old. Making an enemies list might seem, on the surface, emotionally unhealthy, akin to soul annihilation. But, as I'd come to believe, having unburdened myself these last several months of past and present grievances, hates, jealousies, and annoyances, the soul rejoiced in justice, in balance.

Men aren't afraid of making and keeping enemies. Men, for that matter, consider "nice" an insult. They gain power from a rivalry, are inspired by it. Women, on the other hand, tend to be forgiving. Enemies are just in need of healing, understanding, and a hug.

But, as I'd found in my short life as a self-actualized hater, some people didn't deserve the benefit of the doubt, like the Biggest Bitch of All, for example. Just yesterday, she nearly crashed right into me and still didn't acknowledge my existence, even after I said loudly, "Excuse you!" Her name would *so* be in my drawer if I knew what it was.

Maybe 10 percent of assholes are actually puckered kisses

tainted by the stink of misunderstanding. But most of them are just assholes. Understanding does not always lead to forgiveness. Sometimes understanding can make you hate someone *even more.* And yet, universal forgiveness is expected of women, an alleged indicator of our inner goodness. It is unladylike to be pissed off. It is a spiritual failing to count your enemies along with your blessings. Or is it? Back in the day, God Himself was quite the angry smoter, after all.

By the Ides of March, the air was warming, and the nights were getting longer. I decided to do a little pre-spring cleaning. The emotional kind. My desk drawer was cluttered with secret old grudges. Time to empty it out, take a look at what was inside, and make merciless decisions about which grievances to keep and which to let go of.

I opened the drawer, my fingers finding the first scrap of paper. I unfolded it to see . . .

Frieda, a Mega-selling Famous Novelist

She wasn't always famous. When I first met her, she was a newspaper reporter, just another hack journalist like the rest of us. She sold her first novel and asked me to give her a blurb, a two-sentence endorsement of the book. Why me? I'd had moderate success with *Smart vs. Pretty,* an early chick-lit novel.

I read Frieda's debut. I liked it, sent a blurb. The book came out, and exploded. It was an instant bestseller, considered sui generis, a new women's fiction category in and of itself. I was *not* under the erroneous opinion that my blurb had anything to do with the book's success. Frieda had collected better blurbs from bigger fish. The novel was excerpted in major magazines, reviewed positively in high- and lowbrow newspapers. Critics and readers fell in love with the book's plucky big-hearted heroine. Went without saying, I was insanely jealous. Me, and thousands of other authors.

Flash-forward a few years. Frieda's second novel had been an even bigger hit than her first. With only two books under her belt, she'd become one of the biggest stars of contemporary fiction. Maybe the biggest. Movie deals, TV development deals, foreign translations in dozens of languages, tremendous wealth, gigantic fame, legions of fans, and critical respect. A friend invited me to tag along to a party celebrating the release of Frieda's third novel, which was expected to break sales records.

The party was in the penthouse of a swank Manhattan hotel. The balcony views up and down Broadway made me dizzy. Food was abundant on buffet tables. Cocktails were mixed at three open bars. A giant video screen showed, on a continuous loop, the trailer for the Hollywood movie based on Frieda's second novel. Guests received goodie bags with books and T-shirts, all of it paid for by corporate sponsors and the publisher.

My last book party? In my pants. Everyone came.

The crowd at Frieda's fête—booksellers, agents, editors, writers, reviewers—stood around blinking at the spectacle. This was the mountaintop of publishing. A typical book party for a third novel was a dozen friends gathered at an indie bookstore to sip cheap wine in plastic cups. I watched with awe and envy as Frieda made the rounds. When she circulated over to me, I congratulated her and asked, opportunistically, if I could send her my upcoming novel for possible blurbage. She said, "Of course! I'd love to read it."

The novel in question, *Hex and the Single Girl,* was my fifth chick-lit novel. I loved my kooky sexy stories, relished every naughty minute of creating them, sprang out of bed to write, and felt like the luckiest bitch in the world. Large numbers of readers, alas, weren't as tickled by my novels as I was. My track record for the previous four: hit, hit, total miss, near miss. My trajectory as a chick-lit author? Flatlined. The next one had better be a hit, or I was in trouble. My editor had been sending worrisome signals.

Like boyfriends, I believed every novel would be my last. Sales for my most recent—*The Girlfriend Curse,* an award nominee, best reviews I'd ever had—were "disappointing," the scariest word in book publishing. I'd vowed to make a major push for *Hex,* do whatever I could. Although I'd blurbed dozens of other authors, I always felt shy about soliciting quotes for my own books (my old aversion to showing any sign of weakness or asking for help). For *Hex,* I had to swallow my pride and do it.

Yes, I committed a social faux pas by asking Frieda for her endorsement at her party. But a blurb from her could make all the difference. And she didn't seem put off by my request. On the contrary. She seemed fine with it. My relief was tidal. My heart opened to Frieda, and I found myself feeling genuinely glad for her success. I hoped a little bit of it would rub off on me.

The next morning, my editor sent her a manuscript and the necessary info about where to email a blurb. Then we waited. And waited. I sent a few "just checking in" emails. Frieda assured me she'd received the manuscript and would get right to it. Weeks went by. Months. The last-call deadline for blurbs fast approaching, I emailed Frieda's agent, whom I'd met once. Apparently Frieda had been very busy traveling and might've left the *Hex* manuscript in one of her other houses. I bit my lip until it bled, and then volunteered to overnight another manuscript to whichever of her houses she was currently residing in. The agent promised to make double sure that Frieda got it. In the meantime, she wondered if I'd be so kind as to blurb the second novel of one of her other authors.

I replied that it would give me multiple orgasms to do anything she wished. I would have blurbed a gum wrapper for some quid pro quo action. I read the manuscript and supplied a quote within days. I liked the zesty novel. I gave it an honest review. But I had ulterior motives.

Another month went by. The deadline for blurbs came and went. Not a word from Frieda.

I hunted through my bookshelves to find the copy of her first novel, just to make sure I hadn't conjured a false memory of having once helped her. Yes, there it was. My blessing appeared on the book's dust jacket. I opened the cover, and a card dropped out. I'd forgotten Frieda had sent a thank-you note. It read: "Dear Valerie: Here—at last!—is a finished copy of [title of book]—and my heartfelt thanks for giving me my first quote! If you ever need a favor from [industrial northern city], please don't hesitate to ask . . . and thanks again for your help."

It suddenly occurred to me that this note and its loopy signature might actually be worth something to a rabid Frieda fan. (FYI: soon to be open for bidding on eBay.) But her words? Her promise? Her gratitude? Not worth two cents.

Four months, I waited. Four months of sending her loving, patient thoughts, telepathic gentle reminders, struggling to convince myself that she'd come through. Four months of clinging to hope that my furious fretting had been wasted energy, that her quote would lift *Hex* out of the chick-lit glut and save my livelihood and dream.

If Frieda had sent *any* response, I wouldn't have put her name in the drawer of reckoning. "Dear Val: I despised your book. It's an abomination. The handwork of Satan. You defile nature with your filth. I'm disgusted that a single tree died to produce the pulp this accursed trash was printed on. I spit on your family, Frieda." *That* would have thrilled and delighted me. I'd have welcomed excuses, too. "Dear Val: I never got a chance to read your book. I am simply too busy living the life of my dreams. So sorry. Better luck next time!" *That* would've made me weep with gratitude and relief. Any end to the waiting and wondering would have been deeply appreciated.

I reminded myself that she wasn't my friend. I'd met her, what, three or four times? She was an acquaintance. We hadn't signed a reciprocal blurb agreement. She probably had just forgotten about my request. As well as the half-dozen emails we'd exchanged about it. And the emails from her agent. And the two copies of the manuscript on her night table(s). Gee, Frieda sure was forgetful. She might want to see a doctor about that.

Fortunately, I hadn't squandered all my efforts on her. I'd scored excellent quotes from three brilliant writers, bestselling authors whose novels I rushed to the bookstore to buy. Their endorsements gave me comfort and hope, temporary relief from worry.

Those three blurbs, some great reviews, and a twelve-copy floor display in bookstores amounted to meager sales. Readers just weren't buying *Hex,* nor hardly any other pink-covered literary confections. Except for a handful of authors (including Frieda), chick lit was over. Fans were bored of cheeky urban love stories. They lusted for something new—as it turned out, horny vampires and the women who loved them. (Honestly, who could blame them?)

I wrote one more chick-lit novel, as per my contract. And then my publisher cut me loose. Having watched the axe falling in slow motion for over a year, I found that the blow didn't hurt as much as I'd anticipated. It stung. I won't lie. I'd worked with the same editor for six books. When our business relationship ended, it felt like a personal rejection.

Over a soggy summer, I plotted what to do next.

Rebecca said, "Start writing."

"Another novel?"

"Doesn't matter *what*," said Rebecca. "Just sit in front of the computer, and see what comes up."

What came up was a series of magazine articles: a service piece about how body image affects women's sexuality, an essay about my life as a chronic dieter, another essay about ridding myself of fear-of-looking-fat camera shyness by posing nude for a professional photographer, and a reported piece about negative body talk, the internal monologue of self-criticism. Although I didn't see it for a while, eventually the common theme of these articles became obvious. My subconscious had been very busy pointing me in a direction I needed to go, not only professionally, but personally, emotionally. I'd forgotten that an ending could lead to an exciting new beginning.

Flash-forward two years. I was at dinner with my agent, Nancy, and my (exciting new) book editor, Jen, discussing potential blurbers for a brand-new book—a memoir about my lifelong struggle with bad body image—on the verge of release.

Jen said, "What about Frieda?"

I spit my martini across the table. "*Definitely* not her."

Jen sent her a copy anyway. Which, if she ever received it, she completely ignored, as I expected.

Flash-forward *another* two years. I was reading Frieda's review of a binge-eating memoir by a famous food critic. In the last paragraph of her review, she recommended my memoir as a complementary read.

I called Rebecca, told her. "Do we still hate her?" she asked.

Well . . . I certainly appreciated the plug, and was glad Frieda had liked the book. But my feelings about her remained the same. My perspective, however, on those four months of waiting for the blurb that never came had changed. Although Frieda was the focus of my anxieties, she had nothing to do with their root cause. Obsessing about her was a diversion, a ploy of my subconscious to keep me from thinking about my real problems. It was easier to fixate on that stupid blurb than to face an uncertain future and my fear of failure. I couldn't avoid the reality forever, though. It came, and I was forced to reach for the most important tool in my belt: resilience.

"I still hate her," I said to Rebecca. "Her last book sold a million copies!"

But she was off the enemies list. Her career was impervious to the power of the drawer anyway. I tore up the paper with her name on it. I was over it—and her.

Next folded-up scrap:

George, a Boy in Lucy's Class

This piece of paper dated back five years, to when George and Lucy were in kindergarten. They're both in fifth grade now—

and not in any classes together, thank God. What could a then-six-year-old have done to earn a place in the drawer of doom?

This kid, this cherub-faced little boy, for the sake of his own entertainment, sent Lucy's life into a tailspin. And Lucy was already in the middle of another crisis.

Most preschoolers' thoughts center on Mommy, juice boxes, and playdates. They understand the agony and the ecstasy of life via skinned knees and birthday cakes. Lucy's life was a bit more complicated. She'd been hospitalized twice, had had debilitating surgery, was temporarily wheelchair bound, and had been diagnosed with a chronic neurological condition. She'd watched her father die of cancer and grieved for him before she knew how to speak. She'd bravely opened her heart to Steve. At our wedding, she gave an articulate speech about love lost and found that brought everyone in the tent to tears. By six, Lucy had experienced death, grief, physical and psychic pain, renewal, recovery, joy—more of life's bittersweetness than the average thirty-year-old. Her art teacher once chased me down at school to remark on the eerie sophistication in Lucy's drawings.

"It's as if she knows more about life than a typical first grader," she said.

I said, "Thanks," thinking, "You have *no* idea." Despite her trials, Lucy was the sunniest, most trusting and loving person I knew.

When she was in preschool, Steve and I were informed by her teachers that Lucy, alone in her class of twenty, could not attach sounds to the letters of the alphabet. Even after one-on-one coaching, she drew a blank when asked to make the sound for the letter B, for example. She was stumped. Her teachers gave us a thick packet of worksheets to go through over the summer so she could catch up with the other kids.

Lucy's ineptitude was upsetting. She was clearly a smart kid. Her imagination was boundless. If you asked her to tell you a story on the fly, she'd weave twisting plots and subplots involving dozens of characters in multiple settings. Her memory? Freakish. She could see a movie once and recite back nearly all the dialogue. Lucy had the power of observation. We'd walk down the street and she'd point out a shoe in a tree, a single balloon hundreds of feet in the air, a cat in a fifth-story window, a lost earring deep in a crack in the sidewalk. One of her nicknames was Eagle Eye. As we came to learn later, her talent for spotting what other people missed was a symptom of her particular type of ADD. She could see every tiny detail of every single tree. But the forest? The big picture? A blur.

Despite our efforts over the summer, Lucy struggled with phonics and simple math. A month into kindergarten, she was far behind the others. Steve and I were called in for a meeting with the school shrink and kindergarten teacher. They'd both spent hours observing Lucy in class. She would sit staring at the whiteboard, apparently absorbed by the lesson. But when she was asked to repeat what was just said or answer a question, she snapped back to reality, clueless about the last twenty minutes. She'd been off somewhere.

I knew where. Lucy had been in Shrub Town, a land of her invention, populated by heroes (blue and pink fairies, unicorns, friendly sea monsters) and villains (zombies and wild boars). They spoke Shrubbish, and lived under the benevolent rule of their queen, Miss Fluffy, a giant magenta dog, among elaborate topiary and hedge sculpture as far as the eye could see.

Bizarre? Strange? You bet your ass! Steve and I encouraged Lucy's fantasy life, and were proud of her wild imagination. I knew it was one of her greatest strengths.

But, as the shrink and teacher told us, Lucy had to check into reality *some* of the time. She had to learn to read and make change for a dollar. The brightest imagination in the world was useless if it isolated her from her peers. Which, they told us gently, it had. Lucy was having trouble making friends. Kids found her odd and confounding. They said "potato," and Lucy said "vampire babysitter." We agreed to let the shrink run some basic tests on our daughter. Then we agreed to more testing with a child psychologist in Manhattan.

The first thing we learned about being the parents of an ADD kid: Everyone had a very firm opinion about Ritalin. I had a firm opinion about it, too. "Overprescribed! Cocaine for kids! A crutch for lazy parents! Under no circumstances would I ever put my kid on drugs."

"No circumstances" turned out to be the day after three different shrinks gave Lucy the same diagnosis and prescription. Howie had done a *JAMA* search on the long-term negative affects of Ritalin (none). I researched the drug as if I were reporting an article on it. I tried to stay objective, like a journalist, and not freak out, like a nervous parent. I spoke to experts, culled the info I'd gathered. Steve and I went over it all and made the decision.

It was *extremely* hard not to hate—with a throbbing passion—people who took it upon themselves to inform me that firm discipline, fresh air, fish oil, and pixie dust could cure a neurological disorder. Behavior modification did not cure ADD. Drugs didn't cure it either. Like most medication, Ritalin merely treated Lucy's symptoms. And it helped. Like, a lot.

After two months on Ritalin, Lucy could read and make change for a dollar. She caught up academically. But socially? No dramatic improvement. The other kids still found her weird. Steve and I took her to a classmate's birthday party at a play space in the city. Heartsick, the two of us watched her go up to a couple of girls and ask if she could play with them. They told her to go away. She approached another kid, suffered another rejection. Eventually she gave up and played in a toy house—happily, it seemed—by herself. She said later she didn't care about being alone. But we cared. It was agony to watch the repeated rebuffing.

We believed that keeping Lucy's medication a secret would further isolate her. We didn't want her to feel ashamed, either. A diagnosis of ADD was a big deal. She should be able to talk about it. Her teacher agreed, and made it seem like a special privilege for one of her classmates to accompany Lucy on her daily trip to the nurse's office for a midday dose. Any break in routine was desirable, so the other kids clamored to be Lucy's escort. That helped, too.

Getting back to George, the hellspawn.

For show-and-tell, Lucy brought to school a photo of herself, Maggie, Steve, and me cutting the cake at our recent wedding. It was a beautiful cake, three layers of chocolate basket-weave frosting with purple and blue flowers. The real focus of Lucy's presentation was the splendid dessert, how she had three pieces and fed four more to my parents' dogs.

During question time, George asked Lucy how it was possible that she had attended her own parents' wedding. After all, most parents got married *before* they had children. Lucy explained that Steve was her stepdad, and that her first dad, Glenn, had died when she was almost two.

I could understand how some kids might've been confused. Lucy had just described a heartbreaking personal loss, and yet there she sat, smiling, talking about cake.

George wasn't buying it. He asked Lucy what Glenn had done for work. Lucy said she wasn't sure, but he wore a suit and carried a briefcase. That was evidence enough to George that Glenn was not actually dead, but was a secret agent, a spy who, at this very moment, was walking the streets of a foreign city in his black suit, carrying that briefcase full of classified files. This kid had an imagination, too.

Lucy insisted that Glenn was really and truly dead. She'd been to his funeral. She'd visited the cemetery and seen his tombstone many times. George said that the funeral had been a fake and the grave was empty. In love with his story, he repeated it often, to Lucy and the other kids in their class. When Lucy insisted that Glenn was gone, George cast aspersions on Lucy's memories. Everyone knew she was on drugs, after all.

Lucy was too trusting. She started to wonder. Had she—had we all—been fooled? Was her father alive out there somewhere?

I picked her up at school. She was uncharacteristically quiet on the walk home. After her snack, she asked, "Is Glenn really dead?"

She could have said "I'm pregnant" and I wouldn't have been more shocked.

I pried the full story out of her. Finding it necessary, I presented contradictory evidence to George's theory. I pulled out the few photos of Glenn during his decline. I showed her the last video footage of him, ashen-faced, losing his hair, taken early on in the cancer fight when he could still walk. On the phone, Howie and Judy reinforced the truth to her. We drove to the cemetery in Queens. Steve had never been; he'd wanted to pay his respects for some time.

I called the kindergarten teacher. She knew about the situation and had been trying to contain it. She must have called the parents. The next day George apologized to Lucy. Lucy accepted, but she smartly, privately, declared George her sworn enemy for life.

Which was fine by me. I applauded Lucy for starting an enemies list at such a tender age. Why should she go within two hundred feet of a child who was, at six, a fire starter? Last year, in fourth grade, George spearheaded the creation of a popularity index, and purposefully put the girl who'd rejected him at the bottom, reducing her to tears.

I shuddered to think what this boy would be like at thirteen. Feeling confident that his reckoning would surely come in junior high, I tore up his name, too.

Mary, a Mom from the Neighborhood

One day, not long ago, I was walking down Court Street in Brooklyn Heights, minding my own business. I saw a familiar face coming toward me. When we were close enough, I smiled and said, "Hello, Mary."

She smiled and said, "Hello, Rivka."

In all fairness, Mary didn't say "Rivka." For emphasis, I've substituted a super-duper ethic name. Mary actually used another name, unmistakably Hebe, that of the *other* Jewish mother in our daughters' grade at school.

Granted, she did not say, "Hello, Kike," and then slap a gold star on my sleeve. But she'd put that other mother and me on the same mental Rolodex card, the one filed under *B,* for "Big Fat Jew."

The real Rivka and I were easy to tell apart. She was corporate. I was freelance. We both had dark hair, but in totally different cuts. We dressed differently. Rivka was ten years older than me. We traveled in different circles. Well, Rivka traveled; I barely left my apartment. She was an observant Jew, kosher; her husband wore a yarmulke. I was a secular Jew. We didn't belong to a temple. I certainly didn't cover my legs or head.

Mary and I had some social overlap. We shared a few mutual friends and attended a couple of the same dinners and events. Our daughters were (briefly) on the same sports team. Mary had read a few of my books, in which my name (not Rivka) appeared on every other page.

Her husband had seen one of my titles on Mary's night table. Hammered, he stumbled up to Steve and me at a party and slurred, "I know who you are! You write those silly, silly novels." He went on to expound on the stupidity of romantic fiction. "It's for bored, sexually frustrated housewives," he declared.

"Isn't *your wife* reading Val's book?" Steve egged him on, just to see how far he'd go—which was about fifteen feet to the bar for round seventeen.

A few days later Mary apologized on her husband's behalf. I assured her I wasn't offended. I'd heard far, far worse from critics. Besides, soused middle-aged gonads weren't exactly my target audience. "I thought it was funny," I told her honestly. It had been a classic stumbling-drunk comedy scene in the W. C. Fields tradition (minus the wit). This guy could've slurred *anything* and we would have laughed.

But for Mary, an intelligent, warm woman I'd enjoyed talking to, I had higher standards.

"Hello, Rivka," she said.

Hello, scrap of paper with Mary's name on it, right into Jewey Hymiesteinowitz's desk drawer.

Paranoia? Not really. Anti-Semitism—even in my liberal neighborhood—was out there. Sometimes it was overt. Two years ago, a Nazi sympathizer was arrested for stockpiling guns and bombs only a few blocks from my building. Swastikas were spray-painted on local temples and cars. Just last month, flyers were found littering the streets of the Heights and a few other Brooklyn neighborhoods with the words "Kill the Jews." *Just last week,* a box with a swastika on it was left on the doorstep of a local Jewish-run business.

Subtle anti-Semitism was easy to detect if you listened for it. At a holiday party I overheard a blueblooded blonde comment to her husband, "Jewish women are very well dressed." Her husband followed up with, "And they give good head."

True. But, still.

At the café on the corner, while waiting to buy coffee, I listened to a trio of mothers complain about "all these goddamn bar mitzvahs. There's one every weekend. And of course *they* prefer cash instead of a gift."

Also true. And smart!

I always felt a nagging suspicion that when Bess McWhitey

laughed at my jokes, she was thinking, "Jews are funny!" Racially conscious people would bite off their tongues before saying "uppity" or "boy." But other code words—*pushy, vulgar, cheap*—were fair game. Of course, a pushy, vulgar, cheap Jew could throw around those words herself, about herself. She could shout them from the rooftops! While fiddling and doing the hora.

One small slip—okay, a medium-size slip—did not mean Mary hated Jews. Some of her best friends might know people who happen to be one quarter Jewish. But the slightest smack of anti-Semitism, even to a lobster and Christmas lover like me, gave me a hit of the primal defensiveness felt by Hebes all over this great land of ours. Orthodox to sacrilegious, American Jews were vastly outnumbered, deeply misunderstood, and, speaking for myself, nowhere near as wealthy as we were thought to be.

Besides that, Mary calling me by that other woman's name was just plain insulting. I mean, the real Rivka was so much fatter than me.

Ah, what the hell? I ripped up the scrap with Mary's name on it. I didn't need a paper reminder that educated people could also be semiconsciously prejudiced. Plus, the power of the drawer might be overkill. She was stuck with that husband. She should've married a Jewish man. They don't drink.

And we have time for just one more . . .

Ilene, a Veteran Women's Magazine Editor

I'd known this women casually for many years, a purely professional relationship, to say "hi" in the elevators at Condé

Nast, where we both used to work. She included me in her mass emails updating friends and colleagues about her career moves. We had dozens of mutual contacts in the world of women's magazines. Ilene was widely considered to be a hardworking wordsmith with integrity and vision. She possessed the rare talent of being both a macro *and* micro thinker. Although she never held the big job, editor in chief, her reputation as a "number two" was unassailable.

Until now.

One day, I ran into Ilene at a book party. We chatted. She had just started a new job at a successful magazine for women in their forties. She knew I'd been doing a lot of stuff for one of their competitors, but she asked, "Can you come play with us? Please?" which I thought was kind of funny and very flattering. I said I'd email her, and then we were pulled away by other people.

The party was for a friend of ours who'd edited an anthology to which I'd contributed an essay. The party was in January 2009, a big winter for me. My body image memoir had come out a few months before and was doing well. The guide to plastic surgery I had co-authored with Joan Rivers was just out. Joan was appearing on TV shows to support the book, and she always mentioned my name and gave me props. She told radio host Leonard Lopate that I was "a wonderful girl," for which I will be eternally grateful. It would probably be the last time anyone called me a "girl." In reviews of the anthology, my essay was often singled out, mainly because it was one of the few comic-relief pieces in an otherwise serious and intense collection. All those shout-outs and positive reviews, naturally had blown up my ego to Madonna proportions. I was sizzling! My professional temperature usually hovered in the barely above freezing range. I wasn't unaccustomed to the heat, but I liked it. I let myself believe it would last.

And it did! For three months I spent most of my time in the spotlight doing interviews and writing guest blog posts to support my new releases. And then, as suddenly as they sprang to life, the flames went out. My starry vision cleared, and I realized I hadn't done any paying work *for months*. Even worse, I had nothing lined up. With a jolt that turned my innards to liquid, I realized my critical mistake. Even if I did secure a few assignments, like, yesterday, I'd have to write the article (a few weeks), then wait for the piece to be read by editors (up to two months), do a revise (a few days), and bide my time until the check arrived (a month later). This was standard operating procedure. From the minute I got the go-ahead to write an essay (perhaps "The Stressed-Out Life of an Alpha Wife") to the minute I found the check in my mailbox, *four months* might elapse. I didn't have four months' expenses in my checking account. I would have to get something going at lightning speed. Women's magazines moved like glaciers. Sometimes simply getting approval on an pitch—a paragraph describing your idea—could take months.

In no other biz were you expected to do all the work up front, wait months for feedback, do a revision (again, not seeing a dime), and wait months more for a check—maybe. The editor could always change her mind, decide she didn't like the idea or the execution, and pay the writer a "kill fee," or a percentage of the agreed-upon amount. When I was an editor at *Mademoiselle*, the worst part of the job was telling a writer she would receive 25 percent of her fee despite having done 100 percent of the work. This was the main reason I'd quit. I didn't have the stomach for it. As a writer, I faced getting killed every time I took on an assignment. Sometimes I had to do a tremendous amount of work before I was even offered a contract.

Quick horror story: The article idea was couples compatibility testing via handwriting analysis. The editor asked me to find ten married couples who were willing to participate, collect their photos, and send them to her. Based on attractiveness and "the mix" (read: racial diversity), she and her bosses would pick five of the ten couples for the article. It was my job to inform the rejected couples that they were out. Next, I had to get bios and photos from several handwriting experts and submit that material for selection. *Then* I had to write a pitch about the article, provide names and backgrounds for all the sources, and describe how the piece would appear on the page. When *that* was approved, I would get a contract.

I agreed to their terms. The work-to-reward ratio was poor. But I was young and broke, and a byline in a major magazine would have boosted my career. I'd also convinced myself that even though it was a ton of work, and not a showcase for my writing, a big package would be proof that I could make things happen.

Somehow I persuaded a dozen couples to participate in the article, got their pictures, and wrote short bios on each pair. I sent the portfolio to the editor, expecting to hear from her in a week or so. But I didn't get the call for . . . wait for it . . . *two years.* During that time, the couples kept emailing me, asking

what was up, could they have their pictures back? (This was before digital photography. The photos they'd given me might've
been the only copies.) I apologized for the month's bottleneck,
the six months' hold up, the one-year delay, and felt like a bigger idiot each time. I left "just checking in" voice- and emails
with the editor frequently, and she either ignored them or rushed
me off with a flat "no update." After a year and a half, I gave up.
I told the couples the piece was dead and that I was trying to get
their pictures back.

Time passed. One day, I answered my phone and nearly
hit the floor when this editor identified herself. "Long time!
How *are* you?" she asked, as if we'd just spoken yesterday.
Did she apologize? Why would she do *that*? She was calling
with . . .

"Great news!" she sang. "We've decided to schedule the
couples handwriting-compatibility package for December. We
need you to pull it together in the next couple of weeks."

I was speechless. I might've gasped.

"Are you there?" she asked.

"Have you lost your *mind*?" I asked. "You stonewall me for
two years and now you want me to drop everything to work
on this stupid story? I don't know where half these couples are
anymore. I never even had a contract." Plus, it really was a
preposterous article. So what if it'd been my idea?

"Are you saying you're unavailable?" she asked.

"I'm saying, *I'm promising,* that I'll never, ever, under threat
of violent death, work for your magazine again."

Proof of just how desperate I was in the winter of 2009:
I actually considered calling an editor at that magazine for an

assignment. Thank God I didn't, or a tiny part of my soul would have died. I did call editors at every other magazine I'd ever worked for, and was not exactly warmly received.

The Great Recession was upon us. The Dow Jones Industrial Average was at a ten-year low. Unemployment was at 10 percent. The American auto industry crashed and burned in the early months of 2009. The other major U.S. industry devastated by the recession: print journalism. Large newspapers were closing daily. Glossy magazines were going under or shrinking. Rumors abound about this or that legendary magazine's imminent demise—some of them true. Blogs listed "Death of Print" casualties, magazines and newspapers that had folded. A lot of talented people were fired. An editor sent a mass email: "This morning, I was told my services are no longer required and to clean out my office by lunch. I'll let you know where I go from here, but right now, security is waiting to escort me out of the building." Staff head counts were frozen or reduced. Freelance budgets were slashed, expense accounts cut off.

For the first time in the history of magazine publishing, there was no such thing as a free lunch.

Articles appeared—on the Internet—predicting that paper-and-ink newspapers and magazines would not exist in five or ten years. As a fan and reader, I found the idea of life without magazines a sad, sorry shame. No newsstands with all those glossy covers smiling at me? My kids growing up without the smell of ink and perfume strips? Turning silken pages in the tub or on the toilet? Who wanted to use a computer for bathroom reading? I felt a sentimental loss. And the professional threat.

Young writers and editors agonized that their careers were over before they'd begun. Veterans feared they were too old to reinvent themselves. But those worries were for the near-distant future. I needed cash *now*. I had to get jobs from the magazines that were still standing.

Like softballs into outer space, I pitched. I sent emails, made phone calls, spent hours staring at the wall trying to think up article ideas with traction. No subject was off-limits. If an editor called and asked, "Would you like to write an article about couples compatibility via handwriting analysis?" I would've replied, "Nothing would please me more!"

One of the stories I was peddling around town was a first-person wife's perspective on her husband's vasectomy. In pitches, I dangled the drama of Steve's and my ambivalent emotions (mourning the baby we'd never have together), the service-y bits (local or general anesthesia? open or closed vas deferens? what? to? do?), and the hilarious post-op details (having sex too soon and accidentally popping the scrote stitches; Steve sitting on ice packs; the cowboy walk).

I was willing to serve up Steve's testicles on a plate for an assignment. It had come to that.

My flurry of pitching was met with a lot of noncommittal shrugging and maybe-ing from the usual suspects. I didn't realize until the fourth rejection that I was shoveling my ideas into a black hole. Editors wished they could help, but they weren't assigning at the moment and were trying to use up their articles inventory, pieces that had already been paid for but that hadn't run for whatever reason.

A call came in. "Great news!" said the editor. No, she

wasn't assigning me a new piece. An old one, written and paid for years ago, was on the schedule to run next month, and she needed an update ASAP.

The next time an editor said, "Great news!" I would cover my head.

I decided to expand my pitching circle to editors I hadn't worked with before but who had expressed interest. I remembered that two-minute party chat with Ilene back in the ancient bygone era (two months before), when I was on fire. I emailed her. She replied right away. "I'm excited to hear from you!" she wrote, which nearly made me cry. We scheduled a phone appointment. I promised to be ready with loads of ideas. "I can't wait!" she wrote.

When the time came, I pitched my heart out. We talked for over an hour. She loved ("loved!") all five of my story ideas.

Finally, I thought. *Someone has bitten on my husband's balls.*

Ilene requested—and I slavishly complied—formal pitch paragraphs, which she would personally deliver to her boss, the new editor in chief. I knew and liked her boss. She was my Facebook friend, for one thing. Also, when she'd been editor in chief at a couple of other magazines (on her rise to her current position), I'd contributed articles that hadn't been killed or heavily edited.

So! Things were looking up! If Ilene could get approval of two or three of my five ideas—the way she talked, it was all but a done deal—that would, literally, buy me time. I spent two days writing my five pitches. Not cheap little paragraphs, but page-long mini-essays. I sent them. Ilene asked me to tweak a couple. I did. She said she'd get back to me in a few days.

Twelve months and counting . . .

Naturally, I sent a couple of my patented nudgy-yet-pamby "checking-in" emails. No reply.

It was like waiting for that blurb from Frieda all over again, but worse. My crisis this time wasn't eventual. It was immediate.

Every *other* editor I'd pitched—a dozen of them—had given me the courtesy of a timely no. I had to assume my ideas had failed to excite Ilene's boss. She should have told me! I wasn't made of sponge cake. I wouldn't crumble. Rejection was always better than a blowoff—romantic or professional. When someone was waiting for an answer, it was a genuine kindness to say, "Sorry, but you suck."

One month I gave her. And then I did what I had to do.

Scrap. Scribble. Drawer.

That was a turning point. Over the next few weeks, things started to loosen up. A couple of my pitches were picked up after all. A ghostwriting opportunity presented itself, and I jumped on that. During the downtime, I'd returned to my half-written novel, which I was excited about finishing.

Almost overnight, I'd gone from nothing to do to having too much. In over my head, I could breathe again.

Rebecca said, "You'd better hope Ilene doesn't read this book, or you'll never work for her magazine."

I wouldn't anyway. Clearly they didn't want me. The question: Should I put Ilene's name back in the drawer and put her at risk of severe comeuppance (which hadn't, as yet, come about)? I decided to tear it up instead, believing that, in time, she would get hers on her own. Karma, unlike Ilene, always got back to you.

There were other scraps in the drawer, and I planned to look at every one. I thought it was telling that the first four I pulled out shared a common theme. Disrespect. To me, my family, or my ethnicity. Disrespect was a damn good reason to mark someone for enemyship.

Except taking the scraps out of the drawer made my anger dissolve. It was like opening an Egyptian tomb, the fresh air turning the ancient artifacts inside to dust.

Another dose of unlearning: Contrary to my hater dogma, I was not, actually, preserving dignity by secreting my hate in a drawer or the pages of a red corduroy journal. I was being a coward.

I should have pushed back. I should have been brave enough call the wrongdoers on their behavior. I could have said to Mary, "My name is Val. Not Rivka. You had me confused with that other Jew." I could have called George's parents myself, and complained that their son had mercilessly messed with Lucy's head for his own amusement. I certainly could have flamed Ilene with phone calls and aggressive emails, instead of passively, tentatively checking in. As for Frieda, she was untouchable. But maybe if I'd told people the story of my blurb vigil, which I'd rarely done for fear of coming off pathetically, I might've gotten over it sooner.

Harboring hate had served some purpose, though. It gave me valuable insight into myself, and that was worth holding on to. From now on, if I held a grudge, I'd do so lightly, long enough to air it out and watch it crumble to dust.

I brushed the pile of torn-up scraps into the garbage. It wasn't a sign of weakness to forgive. But I would *not,* as we say here in Brooklyn, fuggedaboutit.

Eleven

. . . .

I Hate Your Kids*

A rare treat: Both the girls had sleepovers at a friend's house. Steve and I got dressed up and went out to a nice dinner. The restaurant, a pricey local Italian spot—candles, intimate small tables—wasn't exactly child-friendly. And yet the party at the table next to ours included a girl, about six, and a boy, eight.

This gave me pause. But, ever optimistic, I settled in and began the important work of deciding between wine and a cocktail. I was leaning toward a vodka tonic, and planned to have at least two. Steve looked handsome (cute), Daniel Craigish, across the table. I rubbed his ankle with my peep toe. He took my hand and massaged my ring finger in a frankly sexy manner.

This could turn out to be a very good night, I thought happily. But my libidinous mood was shattered when the boy at the

*Thanks to gawker.com for the chapter title. Love the T-shirt!

next table started screeching because his beautifully plated pasta didn't taste like Chef Boyardee. The girl, meanwhile, pliéd in the tiny space between our tables. The mother cooed, "Sweetie, would you like to sit down now? Honey?" The kid ignored her and then, incredibly, reached into our bread basket and took a roll. The mom shrugged, as if to say, "Gosh darn kids!" She seemed shocked when, instead of offering a sympathetic smile, I glared at her with fury.

Why, I asked myself, would parents take children to this restaurant in the first place? Did they think they were on a multi-generational double date? Would they soon be discussing the decline of Ridley Scott films or the latest Tea Party antics? Or would they react decisively to stop their disruptive, obnoxious brood from eating off a stranger's plate?

None of the above. The mom and dad just sat there watching their brats with inhuman tolerance. I cast enough daggers at the parents to pin them to the wall. Instead of taking control, they let their kids ruin the meals of everyone else in the restaurant.

If this had been an isolated instance, I wouldn't be so indignant. I'd seen this style of permissiveness countless times before: at school functions, birthday parties, in pediatrician waiting rooms, on the street, in stores, on the subway. Nothing, hands down, was worse than being trapped with an obnoxious child and his weak-willed parent on (all together now) an airplane.

My airplane stories could curl your eyelashes permanently. I must have been born under a curse to be seated near or next to foul and determined in-flight jackanapes. I'm not talking about pedestrian tantrum throwers, screamers, diaper bombers, or projectile vomiters. Poopers and pukers are a dime a dozen. I once endured a brat who kicked my seat with vengeful repetition from New York to West Palm Beach, despite my begging his brain-dead mother fifty times to make him stop. Then there was the little girl who threw broken-up bits of crayon at me from Paradise Island to Newark. The father—a manchild dressed head to toe in New York Giants insignia—looked surprised when I complained. He and his kid both thought it was a fun game, hurling waxy chunks at a complete stranger every thirty seconds. What was wrong with me, the dad couldn't fathom, that I failed to cherish the privilege of amusing his beastly moppet for five straight hours?

On another occasion Steve, Maggie, Lucy, and I were flying to Mexico with my sister and her family to go on a Howie and Judy–sponsored cruise through the Baja Peninsula. Alison, who suffered from fear of flying and claustrophobia, had doped herself heavily for the trip. She customarily reserved an aisle seat (less claustrophobic). Also in her row, in the middle and window seats, was a young couple (of assholes). My sixteen-year-old niece, Anna, sat directly in front of Alison, also in the aisle seat, sharing her row with the couple's two young kids, approximately two and three years old.

I'd flown with Alison before, and knew how panicky she got. The last thing she needed was for one or both of her row mates to jump up every five seconds to tend to the kids in the row ahead, or for the kids to jump up every five seconds to whine and/or wave at their parents in the row behind. It was too much activity, too much jostling, way too much noise for any patient person to endure, much less a nervous flier. The plane hadn't left the tarmac and Anna had already been pestered by the kids to unwrap candy and sharpen a pencil. Alison was strapped in tightly. The plane about to take off, and she refused to switch seats with anyone.

I sat diagonally up from Alison. When I glanced back, she shot me a desperate look. This worried me. It was Alison's greatest fear that, one day, she'd be the passenger you read about in the paper, the one who went bonkers mid-flight, raving to get out and frantically trying to open the emergency door. The parents and their kids were aggravating her already frayed nerves.

I knew she was too polite/absorbed by her anxiety to say something. So I took it upon myself. Leaning across the aisle, I said to the parents, "Your family has two pairs of seats instead of four across. If you paired off one parent and one child, instead of two parents and two children, then you wouldn't have to do so much shouting and bouncing around. It's not fair to my sister to be disturbed or to expect my niece to babysit your kids for the whole flight."

The father glared at me, outraged that another person would dare lodge a complaint about his personal business, even if it interfered with innocent bystanders. The mother nodded as I spoke, perhaps seeing the logic of minding her own small children. But she deferred to her husband, who said, "The kids wanted to sit by themselves."

As if that were a valid explanation. "So your toddlers, who drink from bottles, make the important safety decisions in your family?" I asked.

"Who do you think you are?" growled the father.

"Say the plane goes down," I said. "Should my niece be responsible for putting the air masks on your kids' faces or helping them get to the exit? She's just a kid herself, and a complete stranger. Your seating arrangement is negligent. It might be illegal."

The father looked furious enough to punch me (which would've gotten him thrown off the flight; I thought, "Bring it!"). The mother appeared shamed. Anna broke in, saying she didn't mind. Alison fumbled for her vial and popped another pill.

Maybe I shouldn't have brought up the subject of the plane going down.

Steve thought I was exacerbating the situation. (I got the hint when he hissed "Shut up *now!*" in my ear.) I dropped it, faced forward, seething in rage for the rest of the flight while the kids treated their seats like trampolines and the mother failed to contain them. The father? Fell asleep.

Brats are made, not born. It is a cruel paradox how some parents can both indulge and neglect their children at the same time.

The worst parents use children as their personal pride delivery system. Being proud of your kid is one thing. But rabid sports dads and stage moms are living through their kids and using them to fulfill their own washed-up dreams. *Toddlers & Tiaras* mothers are modern-day Mama Roses peddling their Baby Junes for their own glory.

And they brag about it, too, as if vicarious living were admirable. I've been chased down on the street by moms who forced me to listen to a ten-minute anecdote about their kid's triumph at a gymnastics meet, soccer field, or Mandarin-for-infants class. Once, I was cornered by a mom who gave me a detailed description of her newborn's wondrous poop.

I said, "You should have it bronzed."

The mom looked horrified. Well, she'd asked for it. Why had she told *me*? Not like we were friends (but of course). I didn't send off "I Heart Sharing" vibes. However, I was a contributing editor at *Parenting* magazine. It was possible some moms were under the mistaken impression that writing articles about child development meant that I gave a rat's ass about their kids' snack choices and nap schedules.

Well, I didn't. *No one did,* except the mom, the kid, and (possibly, but I doubted it) the father.

Helicopter mommies, sidewalk stroller hogs, alternadads who brought babies in Bjorns to adults-only zones such as rock concerts and R-rated movies, and purveyors of "child-centric culture" had taken over American parenting and turned millions of otherwise kind, loving people into full-on kid haters. When self-esteem-pusher parents ask, "Why is there a war on children in our country?" they should look in the mirror.

A two-pronged parenting approach is to blame:

1. Their prime objective is to maintain their kids' perpetual happiness.
2. They measure their success by how much their kids like them.

Popularity parenting as such is responsible for "A's for effort," a medal just for showing up, a new car for rehab graduation.

You see the result of this approach in supermarkets, where entitled brats throw food and unchecked tantrums. In theaters, they leave popcorn boxes on the floor and aren't told to clean up after themselves. On playdates, they imperiously demand, "I'm hungry. Make me Bagel Bites."

Permissive moms and dads are what I call BFF (best fucking friend) parents. They prioritize a kid's happiness over courtesy, hard work, moral values, and ethical standards. BFF parents curry their kids' approval like insecure teenagers. The fear of being unpopular prevents them from punishing heathen sprites, no matter how richly they deserve it.

As a hater, I'd be a hypocrite if I weren't open to being despised by my own kids. Maggie and Lucy loathe me plenty when I force them to redo their homework until they get it right, appraise their art projects as "half-assed," and make them scrub a crusted pot or scoop the cat litter. My demands and reprimands have (more than once) inspired Maggie to scream, "I hate you!" and slam her bedroom door on me.

Of course I care when my fourteen-year-old hates me! It means I'm doing something right.

How to suss out a BFF parent? Ask, "Do your children do household chores?" The correct answer is not "Marisol does them."

I admit to selfish motivation for making Maggie and Lucy do chores like wee Cinderellas. One less load of dishes I have to put away. One less sandwich I have to make. We aren't sharing only the work. We're sharing our lives. Once Maggie, Lucy, Steve, and I stood around our bed folding laundry just out of the dryer and laughing as the cats burrowed into the warm pile of clean clothes. This is the type of memory I want my kids to retain. The girls often stood on either side of me at the kitchen counter peeling potatoes. Dinner wouldn't taste as satisfying if they hadn't helped make it. At eleven, Lucy was quite the little foodie. She pensively chewed a forkful of the gratin, and said, "Next time, more Gruyère." We all agreed. There would be a next time.

BFF parents wouldn't dream of making kids fold laundry, or letting them within fifty feet of a vegetable peeler. Those things are sharp! Besides which, putting a child to work would be like asking the dinner guests to set the table. (I do that; no wonder I have so few friends.) One mother told me she thought kids' cleaning their rooms was a waste of their time. They would better spend the time cultivating their talents. From what I'd seen of her kids, their "talent" was to post whiney status updates on Facebook.

Homework enforcement is as anathema to BFF parenting as housework. Instead, moms spare their children the agony of math by "helping." A kid who doesn't do his own work fails tests—deservedly so. Doesn't stop parents from complaining about unfairness. One mom I know railed against a fifth-grade math teacher, saying, "He can't teach! My daughter takes one look at the homework and starts crying. She can't do it! I have to go through it with her every night." Well, maybe if the kid took a *second* look and didn't cry/manipulate Mommy into giving her the answers, she might learn something. They'd both learn something.

An English teacher busted a seventh-grader for plagiarizing his book report on *Catcher in the Rye* from the Cliffs Notes.

The pathetically easy-to-catch rip-off earned the boy a failing grade and a two-week suspension. How did his parents react? Did they punish him for cheating? Ground him? Raise high the shame beams? Of course not! The mother sent a letter of protest to the school principal, decrying the academic pressure of seventh grade and accusing the teacher of having a vendetta against her son. His plagiarism, she wrote, *was the teacher's fault.* I heard from a reliable gossip that when the boy returned to school after his suspension, he parroted his Mom's arguments to anyone who'd listen.

It was hard not to hate the mother. The plagiarist? Loathed him, goes without saying.

Another BFF parenting "tell" is rudeness. The shock on people's faces when Maggie and Lucy say "hello," "please," "thank you," "nice to meet you" with eye contact. "Oh, my God! They're so polite!" people say, as if they've never seen a courteous child before.

One girl in Lucy's class habitually disses her mom at school events, telling her to "shut up" and "go away"—loudly, as if she wants everyone to hear. Once, I watched her hold up an empty cup to her mom and say, "Hello? Refill!" The mom laughed it off, as if her insufferable brat were a miniature Sarah Silverman.

I would have dragged Lucy into the hallway and set her straight about how to ask politely for something and show respect. If Lucy were embarrassed and hated me for it, *good!* But this mom let her kid get away with behavior she wouldn't have tolerated from a dog.

The irony of BFF parenting: By treating the kid like a

friend, parents are setting up their child for peer rejection. No one wants a "Hello? Refill!" friend. Lucy brought home a girl for a playdate, and they played the friend's games for an hour. Then Lucy suggested they switch to one of her games.

"At my house," said the girl, "we do it my way."

"In this house," I said, "we take turns."

The girl was so stunned to be upbraided that she agreed to play Lucy's game, and seemed to enjoy it. She acted almost human for the next hour. When her mother showed up, the kid instantly reverted to Veruca Salt. You could almost hear her screaming, "I want a goose that lays golden eggs for Easter—*NOW*!" all the way home. She was never invited here again.

Her mother probably praised Veruca for her assertiveness. BFF parents gush volcanically over their kids' every belch. The stroke of a paint brush is "Genius! My pint-size Picasso!" Playing chopsticks is "Brilliant! Mozart in training!" A three-sentence scribble about summer vacation is "Poetry! Worthy of Shakespeare!"

At a recent international fair at school, Steve and I strolled through the gym looking at fourth-graders' poster boards and displays about the foreign country of their choosing.

I said to one mom, "I wouldn't have thought a ten-year-old could make an exact replica of the Parthenon with modeling clay."

The mom, a sculptor, said, "I just tweaked it. He did all the hard work himself, my little Leonardo!"

The kid nodded and said, "I am very talented."

I smiled and congratulated them, thinking, *Way to go, Mom. You just turned your son into a liar.*

Self-esteem boosting is not what it's touted to be. It places a kid's feeling good about himself above his reaching for high moral standards. Bernie Madoff and Adolf Hitler had reams of self-esteem, but somehow they managed to destroy the lives of everyone they came into contact with and countless others.

The sculptor mother can heap unearned praise on her son to raise his self-esteem, but a growing number of experts claim that parents have no long-term effects on a child's self-esteem, in either direction. But her son might buy it anyway. One day, he'll venture out of her clutches and discover—the hard way—that he isn't "the smartest, handsomest boy in the whole wide world!" It'll be a long fall, from the roof of the Parthenon back down to earth. In an effort to protect a child from the harsh realities of life, BFF parents make the child vulnerable and defenseless against them.

The "Hello? Refill!" crowd, the plagiarists and crayon throwers, the Veruca Salts and little Leonardos, will one day get the shock of their lives to discover that perpetual happiness is not their birthright. That shirking and cheating won't rocket them to the top (unless their last name is Bush). In fact, the children of BFF parents, having been lied to and raised to be spiteful, selfish, lazy-ass cretins, are more likely to resent their parents later in life. They might find it hard not to hate them.

Lynn, a family therapist, has seen kids grow up in her care. She has the perspective of parenting as a marathon, not a popularity contest. "Be your kids' parent when they're little, and they're more likely to want to be your friend when they're adults," she once said.

In my case, twenty years from now, Maggie and Lucy might be my *only* friends.

My kids aren't perfect angels. They whine, fight constantly, talk back, procrastinate, spend way too much time on Youtube. But when they mess up, do a shoddy job, are badly behaved, they are punished or yelled at for it. When they pursue their passions, practice their instruments, get good grades, and are clever and witty, they are praised and rewarded thusly. It seems so simple! And yet, my parenting strategy has raised eyebrows. I once wrote an article for a ladies' magazine making many of these points. The majority of letters about it were in favor. But I received emails from readers who accused me of being too demanding, and even cruel. They thought I was treating my children like hardened adults. It is a parent's job, they wrote, to shield a child from the scary and upsetting.

Keeping a child in the dark is no mercy or comfort. Secrets build a wall between any two people, especially parent and child. A friend of my mom's went off to camp at age ten and arrived home six weeks later to learn that her mother had died, was already buried. Her father hadn't called his daughter at camp, or brought her home for the end of her mother's life, because he thought she might get upset. This woman, now in her seventies, is *still* upset. The shock and betrayal shaped her life.

I explained to five-year-old Maggie (Lucy was only one) everything that was happening with Glenn's diagnosis and his treatment. If I'd lied—"He's gonna be fine!"—the essential trust between us would've been destroyed. When I started dating Steve, both Maggie and Lucy were in the loop. I kept them informed about Lynch syndrome, all the procedures I'd been having, and the ones yet to come. No matter what

Maggie or Lucy asked—"Do you like my outfit?," "How's my essay?," "Will I have to drink a gallon of that disgusting Nu-Litely stuff when I have a colonoscopy?"—my answer was always the same: straight.

In the realm of haterdom, where I've been stationed for ten months now, most of my anger and jealousy is the by-product of my own insecurities and fears. I've compared myself to more successful authors, social butterflies, and Zen monks, and felt inadequate. But holding myself up to BFF parents and their bratty brood? Makes me feel *great* about myself.

Authentic emotions check. A narrow gap this time: *I am* a good mother. *I think I should be . . .* better?

Of course, there is always room for improvement. Sometimes I do spoil the girls with Urban Outfitters dresses and costume jewelry. Steve and I indulge them culturally, going to any concert, movie, art exhibit, or Broadway show they want to see. Unlike my mom, I repeatedly tell Maggie and Lucy they are beautiful, smart, and funny, which is also the God's honest truth. If that is my worst mistake—I should be so lucky—I am happy to make it.

Twelve

Can't Complain

The emotional shift, thus far, in my year of the bitch, has been both subtle and seismic. My day-to-day life hasn't changed all that much. But negative emotions aren't getting the worst of me anymore. I am less impatient and laugh more. I haven't pulled out a single hair in weeks. A former colleague's memoir was chosen as a Daily Beast–recommended read for the week. The spark of jealousy flared, but it died out quickly enough.

At the gym this morning, a woman hung her purse, jacket, and towel on the elliptical machine next to the one she was using. It was the only open machine. I waited for a minute, assumed she was saving it for a workout buddy. A hot young guy got on line behind me. He pointed at the towel-draped machine and asked, "Is that one free?"

I said, "I don't know."

When I am on the treadmill or elliptical and notice a line forming, I hurry up or cut my workout short because it gives me sympathetic agita to see people waiting. People who go way over the thirty-minute time limit, brazenly breaking the rules to suit their own desires? Make. Me. Nuts.

When the girls were little, some parents would hog a swing for an hour, completely ignoring the playground etiquette of pushing your kid for five minutes and then giving someone else a turn. I'd stand there, trying to act cool, while my blood boiled. Maggie would say, "Mommy, you're squeezing my hand."

But that was yesteryear. Today, I will influence my circumstances, be the master of my anger, and not be its impotent little girl.

So I got on the towel-and-jacket-draped elliptical and said loudly to the selfish woman, "Excuse me. Are you using *both* machines?"

"I'm . . . no," she huffed, not wanting to break her stride.

"I'll ask you to please move your things so I can use it."

"Just one minute," she said.

"I'd be happy to do it for you," I said.

"What?" Her eyes bugged. A stranger touch her precious sweat towel? Unheard of!

"I'll put it right here, against the wall," I said, reaching for her stuff.

"Wait," she said, hitting the Pause button.

She stepped off her elliptical and claimed her things. I was already starting up the machine. The guy who'd been on line? He winked at me, which made my heart fly. The machine hog glared, but I laughed—inside—at her. Fired up for taking action against a selfish cretin, I had a *GREAT* workout.

Feeling smug, I told Steve the story when I got home.

"Congratulations," he said. "You really showed her."

"Thank you," I said.

He said, "It's hard not to hate you sometimes, too."

"How so?" I asked.

"You disobey my commands," he said.

"That might be something you never get over about me."

"You have a habit of eating when you're on the phone," he said. "Especially when you talk to your mother."

Disgusting. I had no idea. "That ends today."

"You watch too much reality TV," he said. "And you let the kids watch it."

"After they finish their homework," I defended. Was it a parenting sin to let the kids watch *Top Chef*? They learned about cooking. And *Project Runway*? Maggie had been inspired to take Saturday design classes at Parsons because of that show. I could see Steve's objection to *The Biggest Loser*. If you've seen one season, you've seen them all. Jillian screaming. Bob doing yoga and saying, "Up here in this house . . ." Contestants crying and whooping. But I couldn't resist it. *The Biggest Loser* called to me.

Steve continued, "I hate your piles."

He meant the books and magazines piled high all over the house. He didn't understand why I needed to hold on to books I'd already read, and hadn't even particularly liked.

"This week I'll cull," I said.

"I hate how long it takes you to put away your laundry." Sorting with speed had been one of my (broken) wedding vows to him. I knew how deeply it bugged him to see the stack on the bench by our bed. The girls were lazy laundry putter-awayers, too.

"I suck," I said feebly.

"I hate how you repeat yourself," he said. "You say the same thing over and over again, as if you don't realize you just said it three minutes ago. 'Did you get the mail?' Two minutes later. 'Did you get the mail?'"

"Maybe if you *answered* the first time, I wouldn't have to ask twice."

"If you *listened* to the answer after you asked a question, then you wouldn't have to re-ask it," he said. "Maggie and I both hate how you start a sentence and then trail off without finishing it."

Because, halfway through, another thought came up, and then I forgot what I was originally talking about.

"These aren't substantial," I complained. "Just lowbrow taste and bad habits. Where's the real hate?"

"This might be a big difference between us," he said. "If I had any real hate for you, I wouldn't have married you."

I found that sweet.

"Although, I really do hate the nagging. And the yelling," he added. "And the complaining."

I did complain—but only about things and people I hated. Granted, that was a lot.

"I *swear,* this week I'm donating three boxes of books and putting away my laundry; I won't watch TV, talk on the phone while eating, yell, nag, or complain."

"What is, you are so full of shit?" Steve said.

Fate called the next day. It was Laura, my editor at *Good Housekeeping,* who wanted to know if I'd like to refrain from griping, moaning, and bitching for an entire week and write about the experience. It would be a "road test" article about the bestselling book *A Complaint-Free World* by Kansas City minister Will Bowen.

Two minutes of research later, I learned that Reverend Bowen's vision of a complaint-free world was not only a book but a bona fide international movement. His theory, in a nutshell, is that if you get out of the habit of complaining, you'll soon find you have nothing to complain about.

That might pan out for novice complainers. I doubted Reverend Bowen had ever been on vacation with a family of kvetchperts. My people can find reasons to complain anytime, anywhere. We are unstoppable. Real quotes: "The Caribbean Sea is beautiful! But the waves. They're a bit loud." Or "Not a cloud in the sky! A perfect day for second-degree burns." Or the classic "I know it's a three-star restaurant, but the food is terrible! And such small portions."

According to Bowen, if you point out to someone else that she is complaining, that is a complaint in and of itself, and a violation of his rules. I'd wager that after two days in paradise with my in-laws, Bowen would break like a little girl.

According to me and mine, "complaining" is just another word for "talking." Bowen prefers total silence to the tiniest kvetch. According to him, complaining itself exacerbates problems, as if griping about a flat tire will somehow empty the gas tank. "When we complain," he writes, "we are using our words to focus on things that are not as we would like. Our thoughts create our lives, and our words indicate what we are thinking. It is vital that we control our minds in order to re-create our lives."

Thoughts create our lives? It sounded suspiciously like the magical thinking found in *The Secret*. Bowen's refinement: Your happiness depends on what comes out of your mouth. The quickest route to tapping into the vast power of the universe—to win the lottery, move from trailer to a castle, cure yourself of illness, lose weight, find a soul mate, or get a blow job from Jessica Alba *tonight*—is to say nice things, or nothing at all. Chronic bitchiness will, Bowen was sorry to say, earn you a life of misery, loneliness, poverty, and shame.

Bowen includes a wrists-on component to his prescription. Each time you gripe, you have to move a purple rubber bracelet (via his Web site, his organization sent out six million of them) from one wrist to the other. The physical reminder focuses your consciousness on the quest. On his first day of not complaining, Bowen switched his bracelet twenty times. Six months of starts and stops later, he finally achieved his goal of going twenty-one consecutive days without complaining once.

I doubted I could go twenty-one minutes. Still, I decided to give it a shot. Going by how much I relished that "I'll ask you to fuck off" moment at the gym yesterday (smiling right now, thinking about the expression on that woman's face), I wondered if I was enjoying being an Out Hater a little *too* much. Bowening might give me ballast and nudge me even closer to striking the perfect emotional balance between assertiveness and offensiveness.

I accepted the assignment. After minor convincing, Steve, Maggie, and Lucy agreed to join the experiment. I had to bribe the girls, offering them a hundred bucks at the end of the week, minus one dollar for each complaint. Since they were expert complainers, I felt assured I wouldn't owe them a dime seven days hence.

Day One

"Can't you move any faster?" I asked the kids before drop-off.

"My laces are in a knot," said Lucy.

"Mom, where's my history folder?" asked Maggie.

"I didn't touch your folder."

"So where is it?" asked Maggie.

"You lost it," I said. "You find it."

Lucy said, "We're going to be late—again."

"Shit, it's raining," I griped.

And so on. I complained ten times getting out of bed. And eight times making breakfast. And another five trying to find my keys. Bowen calls this sort of sotto voce grumbling "ear pollution." Our kitchen was thick with it.

The morning routine—the yelling about time, frantic accusations, grumbling about the weather—was how we started the day. Negative, perhaps, but I'd always thought of it as bonding, a classic American family tableau. If we were smiling and cheerful, would our days be brighter, even in a rainstorm?

We'd already blown this morning.

I got them out the door and sat down to my coffee. Phone. Rebecca calling with news. "So, ready for this? _____ just got fired. She was given notice and told to clean out her desk in an hour." The newly unemployed editor was someone who'd wronged us both, as well as mutual friends.

I said, "I'm sure she'll land on her feet. I wish her well."

On the other end of the line: crickets.

Rebecca asked, "Who are you and what have you done with Val?"

I would have loved to join in, gossip, recount past offenses by the terminated editor, and cackle over her disgrace. But Bowen, killjoy, believes talking about someone behind her back is just a way to boost your own ego.

And the problem with that is . . . ?

"When I point out your faults, then I'm implying that I have no such faults so I'm better than you," he writes. In this way, "Complaining is bragging. And nobody likes a braggart."

'Round here, nobody liked a holier-than-thou Pollyanna who refused to divulge. Or who shot down a good story out of pure nice-spiritedness. Gossip was entertainment, a news update, a bonding ritual—good old-fashioned fun. I thought of the famous Alice Roosevelt line: "If you don't have anything nice to say, come sit by me."

Clearly Bowen didn't understand fun. His version of it might be stringing popcorn-and-cranberry garlands while singing along to a Jonas Brothers song. Not that I was being judgmental! That was probably a variation of complaining I hadn't gotten to yet.

Much as I enjoyed gossiping, for the week at least, I was off it.

I told Rebecca about the new plan. "One week, no gossiping," I said.

"That's stupid," she complained.

Then the conversation stalled. Rebecca was irritated; I felt self-conscious. Bowen was right about one thing: Just as an alcoholic had to avoid his old drinking buddies, I would have to avoid my gossipy friends (e.g., all of them). This did not make me feel happy, healthy, or wealthy. It felt lonely.

Not that I was complaining! I was optimistic that I could refrain, even if I missed out on some truly delicious juicy gossip. I'd have only nice things to say about everyone.

Day-one complaint tally: a hundred, approx. Rubber burns were forming on my wrists.

Day Two

The kids started Saturday morning at each other's throats, fighting over who'd clean up the huge pancake-from-scratch mess they'd made in the kitchen. I couldn't count their complaints about each other ("mean!" "idiot!" "jerk!") fast enough. In two minutes, they each dropped twenty dollars.

I did not intervene. Doing so would be "triangulation," in Bowen's book, "having an uncomfortable situation with someone by discuss[ing] the problem with someone else." It was third party complaining or widening the gripe circle. To avoid that, I had to keep out of the girls' fight and let them sort it out themselves. Which I was genuinely happy to do, until I saw the incredible mess with my own eyes. Batter everywhere. Egg on the counter. Flour on the floor. A full sink of crusty dishes. Naturally I had a few things to say about the condition of the kitchen. After I stopped, I had to move the bracelet back and forth about thirty times before I caught up with my mouth.

Maggie went to her bedroom, slammed the door, and started IMing with her friends to complain about me. Triangulation! Bowen would have frowned on that. But then again, if teenage girls don't vent to their friends about their mothers, they'll surely grow up to be therapy patients—or memoirists (not that!).

I used to feel so ashamed and embarrassed about my mom's criticism I couldn't possibly tell my friends—the few I had— what she'd said or how I felt about it. I believed that would make my shame worse. Instead, I swallowed it. Of course, now I know how wrong that was.

Teenage girls need to vent. I supported Maggie's IMing for that reason only. When she emerged from her room an hour later, she seemed to be in a better mood. Still, I had to remind her that she'd complained, and stared pointedly at her wrist. Since telling her to switch her bracelet was, in itself, a complaint, we resorted to glaring at each other's wrists to signal a switch. Maggie sighed dramatically and moved her bracelet.

Day-two tally: around fifty. Not feeling serene in the least. Uh-oh, better make that fifty-one.

Day Three

I was determined to get through the day without a single complaint, but my resolve was tested first thing. I woke up to find a warm refrigerator. The milk had soured overnight. Steve poured it into his cereal, caught a whiff, and said, "Jesus!"

Did Reverend Bowen approve of taking the Lord's name in vain as a means of complaining?

Holy Christ, son of *God,* no.

I glared at Steve's wrist, and tapped mine with my index finger. He gave me a finger, too.

We'd had the same fridge problem only six months before.

Since the appliance was not repaired correctly the first time, I felt entitled to a free repair. How to explain my reasoning to the General Electric rep without complaining? According to Bowen, a statement of fact delivered directly to the person who can address the issue, expressed in a friendly tone, is fine. I made the call. The GE rep agreed not to charge for the repair (lulled by my friendly tone?), but she couldn't send a repairman for a week.

In my previous life, I'd have expressed my dissatisfaction at great volume and length. But, per Bowen, "blaming" is yet another form of complaining. I took a few deep breaths, practicing patience. Sensei Geoffrey would have approved. This situation was as out of the GE rep's control as it was mine. Had I blamed her for it, she could have, for her own devious pleasure, moved my repair appointment back *another* week. Keeping my frustration under control, I confirmed the appointment, thanked her, and hung up.

I wondered how to tell Steve the no-fridge-for-a-week news in a non-kvetchy way. Bowen recommends positive language choices to replace negative-sounding words. Instead of saying "problem," Bowen recommends "opportunity." Change "setback" to "challenge." Struggle=journey. Enemy=friend (ha!). Demand=appreciate. Complaint=request. "Something was done to me"="I created this myself."

"No fridge for a week," I said to Steve. "What a great opportunity to face a challenge on our journey in the life we create for ourselves."

Steve nodded and said, "I'm seeing a lot of pizza in our near future." Since pizza was his favorite food, this was definitely not a complaint.

The optimistic language felt fake. I sounded like a politician, someone who'd whitewashed a bad situation for selfish gain. The strategy of telling people what they wanted to hear usually worked. Could I bullshit myself? Would I believe my own semantic inspirational soft-soap?

Only one way to find out.

"The fridge is broken," I said to myself. "But would it get fixed?"

Yes it would!

"Could I afford takeout?"

Yes I could!

"Should I let it bother me that my expensive five-year-old major appliance is clearly a lemon and that I can probably expect more breakdowns and aggravation in the future?"

Yes I should!

I mean, *No I shouldn't!*

I tried to drape a metaphorical silver lining across the useless hunk of steel, but feeling happy about a busted fridge was a struggle—I mean, a "challenge." Clearly, I had no future in politics.

Day-three tally: a couple dozen.

Day Four

The only way to get through an entire day without complaining was not to speak at all. I would be as silent as a nun. I kept my lips buttoned when Ollie, one of our cats, hairballed on my handbag. I smiled calmly when Last-Minute Maggie said an art project was due tomorrow and I would have to get her supplies. I nodded when Steve announced he had auditions all day, a rehearsal that night, and would not be available to pick up the kids from school or keep them busy until dinner. I was on tight deadline and I needed the full workday to meet it, which I was not going to get.

Just another opportunity/challenge on my journey, which I appreciated very, very much.

Bowen believes that every bump (perhaps "bounce?") will smooth over if you believe it will. This, I knew, was complete and utter crap. But I took a deep breath and tried to *believe* something would give. Incredibly, it did. Lucy called to say she was going to her friend's house after school. Maggie called to say she and her friends were walking over to the art supply store together. Afternoon suddenly free, I had the extra work time I desperately needed.

By five, my article was finished. I went to pick up Lucy at her pal's house. Her mom greeted me at the door and immediately started complaining about the horrible weather. I nodded, but said nothing. She then asked if I'd heard about a flood on the subway and the long delays. I shook my head—hadn't heard, no—but kept quiet. One last stab, she asked my opinion about one of the kids' teachers, with whom, I knew, her daughter was having a hard time. I shrugged. Obviously slighted by my failure to engage, she hustled Lucy and me out the door. I felt guilty. I'd insulted her by not chatting about local news and events. Not joining in felt meanspirited.

The evening wore on, but I stayed quiet. Maggie worked on her project; Lucy did her homework. I was patient and unflaggingly positive. The strain was killing me.

I got into bed, my bracelet on the same wrist as it was that morning. I'd done it. Instead of pride, though, I felt frustrated and exhausted.

Steve arrived home much later than expected, smelling like beer. Ordinarily I'd have had something to say about *that*. But I kept my mouth shut. As Bowen believes, "a lot of jabbering doesn't improve our time with [partners], it makes it less precious. Silence allows you to reflect and to carefully select your words . . . rather than allowing your discomfort to cause you to spout off a laundry list of grievances."

I wondered if Bowen's wife was a bit of a nag.

He hadn't, apparently, read the study on the dangers of self-silencing in marriage.

Naturally, I was *dying* to say, "Where the &%$#& have you been? And why the &★#$@ didn't you call?"

When Steve got into bed, he braced himself for a barrage of "I" sentences put in the form of a question. He deserved a litany of them for having kept me up waiting, worrying, while he was at a bar with his friends. But I said nothing. Surprised, relieved, delighted, he smiled, kissed me, rolled over, and started snoring. I would have loved to kick him awake and spew venom at him until dawn. Instead, I simmered, wide awake, for an hour. I felt frustrated, helpless, depressed—as if I'd lost my voice. In silent reflection, I concluded that the code of silence might make Steve happier, but it was making me miserable.

Day-four tally: a bitter goose egg.

Day Five

We took the kids out for a movie and dinner. The movie? Stank. It was a sequel, and we had had high hopes. Steve said,

"Well, that was a waste of time and money," and I glared at his bracelet. He rolled his eyes and switched sides.

In Bowen's view, there are critics (bad) and reviewers (good). Critics tear apart a movie or book just to show off how smart they are. Like gossiping, "criticizing can be a form of bragging." Reviewing, however, is informing free of judgment. Naturally, I far preferred punchy, judgmental reviews to rote plot summaries. The complaint-free life seemed designed to suck the fun out of everything, even trashing a lame movie over dinner.

So there we were, sitting at the restaurant after the show, the four of us staring at our Diet Cokes, not letting ourselves say anything interesting. We started eavesdropping on the three people at the table next to ours. One man did all of the talking—about his mother in the hospital; how the mother hated his girlfriend, who wasn't being supportive of him during this difficult time; that his siblings were shirking their duty to the sick mom; and that she was hardly appreciative of his efforts.

It was painful to listen to, not only because the guy's life was a disaster, but also because his complaint-oriented attitude was atrocious. He didn't strike a single hopeful note in his thirty-minute sad song. By dessert, his friends looked like they needed a hospital stay. His negative attitude was clearly making his very real problems worse.

I'd been there myself, of course, with Glenn. During those awful months, though, when I had good reason to, I rarely complained. I bit my lip, found my grit, and did what needed to be done. Instinctively I stayed positive because only optimism was conceivable, given the alternative. *Not* complaining had gotten me through the roughest year of my life. I'd had the strength not to gripe, but only when I had every legitimate reason to do so.

A complaint paradox. When I'd had genuine hardship, being complaint-free came naturally. I was grateful for what was good about my life, when, in reality, our circumstances were bad. Big problems made me appreciative of small blessings. Whereas small problems inspired a super-size impulse to whine.

Major aha moment: For me, complaining was a litmus test. If I felt the urge, then the matter at hand wasn't really so awful. Being melodramatic about a minor problem made a mockery of it, and minimized it to nothingness. *Not* complaining about a major concern was showing it the proper respect, underscoring its gravity and seriousness.

Meanwhile, the guy at the next table was still going, not showing the proper respect for his problems at all. Where was the faintest hint of love for his mother, or sadness about her illness, or appreciation and understanding for his obviously long-suffering girlfriend? He hadn't a word of gratitude for anyone—not the doctors, the nurses, his friends. God, as my witness, I'd never sound *that* awful.

But . . . I longed to sound *a little* awful.

Pretending to be positive all the time? Why would that be any better/different from being negative all the time? During this week of not complaining, I'd felt dehumanized, like a cult member, forcing myself to follow Bowen's group-think theories, his one-size-fits-all prescription for happiness. I'd felt blocked, repressed, stressed-out, decidedly *un*happier—the opposite of the intended outcome. Looking at the slack faces of my family across the table, I saw the horrible truth.

Man, were we boring!

Which was worse: being bitchy or bland?

It was far, far worse, a crime against nature, to willfully force yourself to be bland.

That tore it. I had to end the Bowenization of my family. Honestly, what was the harm of trashing a bad movie or indulging in a little gossip? If I lived in constant fear of saying or doing or thinking the wrong thing, I might as well write my own name on a piece of paper and put it in a drawer. I'd be disrespecting myself.

The fridge? A bummer. The drunk husband? A damn good cause for self-expression. Not enough work time in the day? A problem in need of a solution. A friend with gossip? The only problem there was denying her the joy of sharing her news. A bad movie sequel? An "opportunity" to trash it together as a family.

I said, "Yeah, that movie *sucked*. The story? Pointless. Characters? Unsympathetic. The dialogue? Clunker after clunker. The acting was second-rate, and the popcorn was *stale*. And I'm not switching my bracelet. I'm taking it off and throwing it away."

Steve removed his, too, and said, "Thank God that's over."

Maggie and Lucy peeled off their bracelets and asked in unison, "What about the money?"

"Why don't you spend what you've got left—and it's not much—buying us dinner?" I suggested.

This brought on a swell of complaints, whines, and grievances from the girls that would have eradicated their allotment of dollars in haste. We agreed it was a wash.

Day-five tally: irrelevant.

Day Six

Woke up, cursed the alarm, yelled at the girls for taking for*ever* to get dressed, and felt like myself for the first time in a week.

I give props to anyone who can be complaint-free. But I am not one of those people. I've grown happily accustomed to expressing—with my own choice of words—the good, bad, and *fugly*. Bowen would probably say I quit too soon. I would counter, I went far too long. Not for just the last several days, but for most of my life.

Between wallowing and swallowing, there is a dry middle ground. That was where I planned to go, even if the food is terrible, and such small portions.

Thirteen

Anger Management

W̅hat does keeping hate in a closet get you, in a purely
practical sense?

A Lot of Friends?
Maybe being sunny and pathologically positive will win you
invites and casuals. But who needs 'em? Close friends are like
breasts. More than a handful is wasteful.

A Happy Marriage?
Self-silencing wives who swallow their hate and try to keep
the peace will soon rest in peace. RIP. The *long* nap.

Loads of Professional Contacts?

Some bridges need to be burned. Burned to the *ground*. Better to know your enemies than twist into a pretzel trying to please all the people all the time.

Happy Kids?

Aspiring to be popular with your children will turn you into the worst kind of parent, and them into sullen brats who'll eat cereal on your basement couch until forty and blame you for their stunted lives.

Timely Payments?

As if! I sent my very last weak-ass "checking-in" email last month, a flaccid inquiry, in the old benign nudgy style, to a magazine editor about a late payment. She wrote back that "The check should arrive any day."

Another week went by, my mailbox remained as empty as her promise. Instead of stewing in aggravated silence or sending another milquetoast email, I left voice messages with the original editor, her assistant, the managing editor, and her assistant. Assertively (not the least bit nicely), I said, "I have not been paid for an article currently in print. The check should have arrived six weeks ago. I'll ask you to look into this right away. Thank. You." Within the hour, I received three apologies. A check arrived via messenger two days later. I'm telling you, if I got nothing more out of my year of hating, it was the Zen power of "I'll ask you . . ." Moved mountains with a spoon.

Fast Service?

Being patient and passive is a guarantee of *slow* service. The phrase "when you get a chance" spoken to a waiter translates as "don't bother." Few things make me angrier than poor service and inedible food. I mean, I might as well eat at home. I used to seethe in silence about waiting forever to order or to be served. But that was so last year.

So Steve and I went to a restaurant and the ditzy waitress failed to deliver our cocktails, even after she'd brought the food. I waved at her—assertively.

She said, "Give me one second."

I said, "We've already given you twenty minutes. *I'll ask you* to bring our drinks now, please."

The waitress blinked and said, "Okay."

Thirty seconds later a vodka tonic appeared before me. It never tasted so sweet. For all I knew, the waitress spit in it. I didn't care. I felt like I'd won a personal victory merely by asking for what I wanted.

Steve, born with sensei-level patience, would have waited until we were already out the door before complaining. "You hit the right tone," he said. "Reverend Bowen would have called it a statement of fact." We toasted and talked about serious and important matters, like what to order for dessert.

Laughs?

Take my nice, please. Agreeable is the enemy of comedy, unless you show a saccharine-sweet person strolling down the street and falling into an open manhole.

Making a goddamn nuisance of myself, I was phoning all my lifers to tell them whatever I was feeling and any news I had, good, bad, sad, mad, whatev. I called Tomas and got his wife, Becca.

An avid reader, she asked, "What's on your night table?"

I said, *"American Wife,* by Curtis Sittenfeld. It's pretty amazing."

She said, "I liked *Prep.* Did you?"

I said, "I was too seething with jealousy to read that one."

And she *laughed.* My rank jealousy amused her. "I love that," she said. "I love you, Val!"

"I love you, too!" I said, with disgusting sincerity, which I was getting a taste for.

At a breakfast date with Liza, a casual friend I would like to nurture into a close, we ran into a woman we both knew a little. The woman started blabbing, insufferably, about her son's weekly chess-tournament schedule and recent victory.

When she paused to draw breath, I said, "That's so *great*! He totally deserves it. Good luck to you both."

The woman blinked, gathered herself, took the hint, and left.

Liza grinned and shook her head. "You are so bad," she said.

"Who's ruder?" I asked. "Me for cutting her off, or her for making our ears bleed?"

And she *laughed.* I joined in, and hoped this would be the beginning of a beautiful new friendship.

. . .

I'd been locked in the habit, the pattern, of hiding my hurt feelings. But, as I came to understand, I'd only limited myself. By unblocking the negative emotions, I created a vacuum that allowed trust, love, and true confidence (as opposed to bluster) to rush in.

My doctor told me that the hate in me just had to come out. I followed his orders, fessing up to jealousy, phoniness, coldness, bitterness, insecurity, envy, distrust, impatience, revulsion, pettiness, bitchiness. Name the hate, I let it out.

The big question: Was I happier for it?

I'd say that I was generally more "er" about all of my emotions, which (bonus) made me deep*er*.

There were two variations on the Robert Plutchik Wheel of Emotions. First, the 2-D model, a flat, circular, eight-pointed star shape with a center hub and spokes. The 2-D wheel is an apt metaphor for the cyclical nature of experiencing emotions. To progress, the wheel has to make a complete rotation. Revolve to evolve. Putting the "motion" in emotion. For a long time, my wheel was stuck. I gave it a conscious push, and was propelled toward anger, then sadness, then happiness again. On the 2-D model, emotional progression is sequential, one after the other, distinct, and temporary.

The second model of the Wheel of Emotions is in 3-D. Picture a circular base, the hub of the wheel, with the spokes bent back and fused together to form a point, taking the shape of a cone. The 3-D version of the wheel doesn't rotate in a straight line. It rolls around and covers ground.

On the 2-D wheel, love and remorse (or acceptance and boredom, or serenity and pensiveness) are opposites with a lot of space between them. But on the 3-D model, opposites touch, come together, are fused.

People with high EQ (emotional quotient) experience their emotions in 3-D. They feel things not sequentially (love *then* remorse), but simultaneously (love *and* remorse; *l'amour triste*). *Concurrency*—or all things at once—by the way, is a synonym for *harmony*. If you seek harmony, you can't possibly be happy 24/7. Harmony is the interplay of all your emotions, resounding in a symphony with buoyant and mournful and sprightly and languid notes.

Now, imagine plinking the same single key of a piano day in, day out. Torture! Trying to be happy, day in, day out, hitting that same one note over and over, *does* make you a prisoner of your emotions. Mary T. Browne said as much all the way back in chapter 5.

Now I get it.

The third dimension, the one that turns a wheel into a cone, isn't height. Or width. It's *depth*. Deep, in this case, isn't a depression at all. It's an inflation. To live an emotional life in glorious 3-D, you have to expand, like healthy lungs full of air, and feel all your emotions, all at once. Deep versus shallow? Who cares? A better question is whether I was full with emotion or flat. Which brings me to tenet number one for the rest of my harmonious life, something I never thought I'd ever aspire to: plump it up.

So, the other day, I was walking home from running errands and I saw the Biggest Bitch of All heading my way. She passed a couple of other people first, and pulled a Williamsburg on them. Then, as I watched with amazement, the BBoA broke into a bright smile. I thought my eyes were playing tricks on me, and I stopped to rub them with my fist. Nope, the BBoA *was* beaming. Not at me, of course. The man a few paces ahead of me returned her smile and said, "Hello, Bitch."

He didn't say "Bitch." He used her real name, which turned out to be Old English slang for "vagina." (Henceforth, she will be known as the Biggest Vagina of All.) As soon as the man walked by, the BVoA's smile disappeared. Her eyes returned to the fixed point three inches in front of her nose.

When she passed me, I grinned and waved, elbow tucked in, my hand a queenly quiver. I almost said, "Hello, Vagina."

Did she make eye contact, nod, smile, say, "'Sup?" Nah, she Williamsburged me, as always.

Her persistent, determined snobbery struck me, finally, as so her problem. We all do what we have to do to feel better about ourselves. Apparently, staring at a spot in front of her nose and ignoring plebes who said "hello" to each other made the BVoA feel confident or superior. If she liked to walk around with a stick up her ass, that was her choice, and her business. It had nothing to do with me.

My next-door neighbor, the college kid who hosted parties on his deck? His loudness affected me, but it had nothing to do with me. He wasn't trying to keep me awake. Last time he was out there with his friends at midnight, I said to myself, "Don't take it personally." The explosion of anger never came. I managed to fall asleep, despite the noise, and without an Ambien.

The same application worked to defuse the stress of long lines, traffic, loud cell phone talkers, editors who didn't reply to pitches, incompetent sandwich makers. Even more than practicing patience or finding humor in the situation, not taking *anything* personally cut off my inner rage monster at the knees. Being less of a narcissist (aka, someone who took *everything* personally) did wonders for my blood pressure.

So tenet number two of my harmonious life was: it's not about me.

Steve and I went to see *Clash of the Titans* (eh, I'd give it a B-). Next to us tittered a group of five or six teenage girls. They did not stop talking—at normal conversation volume—during the previews and well into the first act. It was extraordinary inconsiderateness. Steve said, "How can you stand it?"

Usually I made him move if we were seated near talkers. I'd been known to move three or four times before settling in. "They're just idiots," I said.

He couldn't write them off, though, and shushed them. They ignored it. He said, "I'll ask you to please quiet down."

His sentiment was seconded—and thirded and fourthed—by other viewers. The girls' giggling was drummed out by shushes, to the gratitude of everyone in the theater. And Steve could take credit. He seemed proud of himself. My shutting up allowed Steve to find his own irate voice. I needed less rage, and he needed a little more. A symbiotic victory.

Soon after, I was standing on line at Duane Reade with

Maggie and Lucy, along with twenty other people. One open register. A manager walked by. I said, "How about opening another register?" The other customers on line *applauded*.

Lucy said, "Go, Mom!"

Maggie said, "That wasn't too embarrassing."

The manager, sensing a revolt, opened two registers. The customers formed three lines, all of which were short and speedy.

This was a small victory, but a victory nonetheless, for me and the other people who just wanted to get their toothpaste and shampoo and go home. A thousand small victories— paying bills, meeting deadlines, loving my husband, educating my kids, making time for friends—might be a smarter life goal, even more meaningful, than the one I'd been fixated on for so long. Making "it" (define "it" however you'd like) might never happen. But doing the right thing would happen, every day. I'd hold on to my dreams and ambitions. I couldn't let those go if I tried. But fear of failure was better left behind.

I'd been so afraid of not making "it," of coming off badly, of turning into Val Black, of being ignored and disrespected, of disappointment, abandonment, losing love, embarrassing myself, being lonely, getting sick, being wronged, getting old, among so (so) many others. In my mind, anything that scared me turned into a cause for hate. I was terrified about the possibility of getting sick and had somehow turned that into doubt about Steve's caretaking ability, for example. Nine times out of ten, hate is a thin mask for fear. Everyone has real reasons to be anxious. And everyone has his or her method of choice for drowning fear, numbing it, ignoring it, raging against it, and pretending it isn't there. An alternative to disguising my worry with anger was to stand back, stop fighting, and let fear come through the door.

As Americans, we define bravery as fearlessness. A brave person faces the unknown with dry skin and a steady pulse. Dauntless, she'll hurtle toward danger at ninety miles an hour. But is that really bravery—or stupidity? Or sociopathy? Courage isn't a mental disorder. Real courage is feeling afraid—pee-in-pants scared—but hurtling into the unknown anyway. Holding back fear, or anger, or any emotion, is like staying in the same spot forever. You'll have clean pants, but you'll be stuck.

So this was my third, last, and most important tenet for the rest of my harmonious life: take the risk.

My minorly inconvenient hysterectomy was scheduled two days before Mother's Day—which I found ironic, although I wasn't entirely sure why (paging Alanis Morissette)—and one year to the day of my first colonoscopy that changed the lives of everyone in our family forever.

A notable positive shift: the Frankels had bonded over our mutation. Our growths had made us grow closer. Alison and I were seeing each other more, talking more, than in the last few years. My sister was my best and first lifer, after all, and it was great to be reminded of that. She isn't a sentimental person by nature either, so we held back on the "I love you's" and supportive hugs. But the depth of feeling was there, if just below the surface.

A few weeks pre-surgery, the girls and I drove to Short Hills to my parents' house for suburban relief from steamy city April. Judy made a gorgeous vegetarian lasagna for us. Howie opened a bottle of wine. The girls were permitted tiny sips.

"Almost done with my new memoir," I told them. "Don't worry, Judy. You're not in this one, I swear. Well, just a little. As your alter ego, Judy Black."

"Oh, God," she said. "I'm not reading any of your memoirs! I'll wait for the novel instead."

Judy told us about her next assignment in pet-assisted therapy. She'd been taking her golden retrievers to children's wards and hospices for ten years. "I'm going to a facility to participate in a study on the effect of pet therapy on violent psychiatric patients," she said proudly.

"That's brave," I said. "Are you sure this is a good idea?"

"There'll be security," she said. "And I'll have Nick." The dog.

"He could drown an attacker with his drool," I said. A good therapy dog, Nick was too dumb and sweet to protect anyone.

"I'm sure it's safe," said Judy.

"How do you feel about Mom spending time with violent psych patients?" I asked Dad.

He shrugged. "Well, water seeks its own level."

We laughed, Maggie and Lucy, too. Dad was quite proud of his joke, soaking it up. Mom swatted him on his arm, but she was laughing.

A blind woman could have seen the cuteness. I felt deep gratitude knowing that my parents were happy together after fifty years of marriage.

"So we're all coming to Brooklyn on Mother's Day," said Judy, reminding me of the plan. Usually, the family gathered at Alison's on Long Island. "If you're still in the hospital, we'll visit you and take the girls out to lunch. If you're home, Alison and I will bring all the food. You don't have to do anything."

"I should be home," I said. My insurance company had sanctioned a two-day hospital stay only. "Rebecca and Nancy want to have a 'Goodbye, Uterus' party for me. I thought the Evite should say, 'Thanks for the Ovaries.'"

"Who would you invite to a 'Goodbye, Uterus' party?" asked Judy.

"Close friends," I said. "That's all I've got anyway."

Dad said, "Me, too. I've got, like, three friends."

Three. I told them about the quantitative friend studies. Three real comrades was all you needed.

Judy said, "I used to have tons of friends, God, what a hassle it was to maintain them. When you get older, it's easy to see which of your friendships really matter. You let go of the ones that don't. You're happier with less."

"Everything gets easier," said Howie. "You stop worrying about what you should do, who you should be. The war is over."

The war was over. I felt like I'd been through a war this year. It'd started bleakly, in doubt and disillusionment. Despite decades of hard work, life seemed to be getting tougher, not easier. Maintaining a positive attitude, wearing the poker face, had become impossible.

Into this bubbling stew life threw a monkey wrench or two. My good health—something I'd relied on and taken for granted—was suddenly a giant question mark. My ability to earn a living in publishing—which I'd been in constant fear of losing—was seriously imperiled. It wasn't paranoia or a failure of optimism. These were the cold, hard facts.

Facing the reality of my situation, I'd revealed myself to myself, admitting to disappointments, fears, failures, pettiness, and justifiable angers. Ultimately, the process had left me grounded and steady on my feet. I gained a depth of understanding about the roots of emotions that lay beneath the weedy ones on the surface. I knew that this insight would make me happy—some of the time. And sometimes I'd feel adrift, gasping and grasping for a sense of security that even a loving marriage, a handful of close friends, and a halfway decent career would not provide. I'd have moments of doubt. And then the moments would pass. This was my new reality, emphasis on the *real*. And it was a comfort.

That grinding sound? It was the authentic emotions gap closing, good and tight, hopefully forever.

After we finished dinner, Maggie, Lucy, and I cleaned the dishes and settled onto the couch in the den—the site of so many childhood memories—to watch a movie.

My parents would join us, after they sorted out dog feeding, brushing, yard poop management. Their discussion quickly turned into a screaming fight over who bore the heavier burden of caring for their four pets.

"Hey!" I interrupted them. "I thought the war was over."

"The war *is* over," said Judy.

Howie grinned. "But the dogfight goes on."

EPILOGUE

Three weeks ago I was relieved of my uterus, ovaries, fallopian tubes, and cervix. The recovery was both easier and harder than I'd anticipated. Easier, thanks to my few and fabulous friends, who, answering all my needs and desires, sent books, food, books, flowers, more food, and more books (they know me so well), and paid visits to the hospital and our apartment. Steve and the girls were excellent caregivers, especially Lucy, who pressed her attentions whether I wanted them or not. Still, I drank all the tea she made, gallons of it.

Ah, the drugs! I got a morphine drip in the hospital and then a big bottle of Oxycodone to take home. I loved my morphine button, which the nurse called my "special friend." I'd push and push it until I passed out. Morphine sleep = bliss. I left the hospital sore but well rested.

The hard part: My midsection ballooned with fluid. I lost my uterus but looked three months pregnant! So much for the jokes I'd made about "finally having a waist" after my bits were removed. I couldn't zip my jeans, much less button them.

At my one-week postsurgical checkup, my doctor told me that swelly belly was normal, typical, the body's response to trauma, and would go down eventually.

"Eventually?" I asked. "Meaning a few days?"

"A few months at the outset," he said. "But you'll be back in jeans after six weeks."

No sex for six weeks, either. Initially, the last thing I wanted was anyone—including Steve—going near my incision. But after a week or so, I started having hormone-replacement-related libidinous thoughts. Intercourse was forbidden, but we could try outercourse anytime, and did.

I was HAPPY!!! to report that, although most of my sexual organs were gone, my clitoris remained intact, fully functional, and in fine working order.

Afterwards, my husband smiled at me, looking uncannily, *exactly*, beyond cutely, like Stephen Quint, the devastatingly handsome and talented American actor and musician.

"That's a relief," he said.

Steve was a generous lover. My pleasure was his. Fitting his tendency to keep his emotions tucked in, he hadn't mentioned any concerns about how the hysterectomy would affect my libido and response. But he must have been worried about it.

For me, evidence of a healthy mojo was more than just a relief. It was the release of months' worth of keen anxiety. I'd made the mistake of reading some horror stories online about women who, post-op, never came again, hated being touched.

Steve asked, "How do you feel?"

"Like I'm on the other side of a really rough year," I said.

"Next year will be better," he said.

"I feel that, too."

We talked about a couple we knew who had just separated, a high-drama split over a seemingly small misunderstanding. *Seemingly* small. It was the tiny tip of the huge iceberg, packed tightly with decades of repressed anger and resentment.

"Can you imagine how hard this year would have been if we'd been in trouble?" I asked.

"Horrible," said Steve. "I'd take a health and career crisis over a rocky marriage any day."

"I love you so fucking much," I said, sounding as gushy as I wanted to be, fully expecting him to mock me or roll his eyes at the sappiness.

But he didn't. For all his Maine stoicism, Steve has his rare sentimental flashes. "I love you so fucking much, too," he said softly, sweetly, drawing me into a tight hug, which tugged *hard* on my stitches. Hurt like a mofo. But wrapped up in Steve's arms, feeling so fortunate, so lucky in love, about as far from haterdom as I could get on earth, I couldn't, wouldn't complain.

Valerie Frankel
Brooklyn Heights, May 27, 2010

ACKNOWLEDGMENTS

I couldn't write a book about hate without the love of family and friends. I'm eternally grateful that they continue to put up with me despite my obvious emotional shortcomings.

Stephen Quint, you are a man of character, and a damn fine husband. I will always look across the table at you and think, "Cute!"

Maggie and Lucy, my excellent daughters, I love you most when you're annoying the hell out of me. I hope the feeling is mutual. You're both my favorite, and don't ever forget it.

Howie, Judy, and Alison Frankel: Nothing like the discovery of a life-threatening genetic mutation to bring us closer. We got through our Lynch syndrome crisis intact (minus a few organs) as a family. I see many healthy years (and colonoscopies) ahead for all of us.

My friendships are few but fierce (and, of course, filthy). Ann Billingsley, Dana Isaacson, Daryl Chen, Judy McGuire,

Kelley Richards, Nancy Jo Iacoi, Rebecca Johnson, Sarah Tobin, Tomas Rossant, thanks for sharing your lives with me.

It's hard not to *love* my Hater Helpers! It takes a particularly kind, generous, patient, and forgiving person to divulge their thoughts on anger, jealousy, impatience, and resentment. Deep thanks to Mary T. Browne, Joan Rivers, Jane Greer, Laura Carstensen, and Sensei Geoffrey Shugen Arnold. A special holla to Lynn Schlesinger, who I used to think of as my parents' friend but now claim as my own.

Some of these chapters started as magazine articles. I owe tremendous thanks to Rosemary Ellis, Laura Mathews, and Janet Siroto at *Good Housekeeping* for allowing me to complain on their pages. Lucy Danziger, Paula Derrow, and Lauren Purcell at *Self* say yes to nearly everything I pitch, against their better judgment. Thanks for your trust, and for always pushing me to go deeper (Paula).

Jen Enderlin, who titled and edited this book, is the perfect combination of super-genius visionary and raucous drinking buddy. Put a few margaritas in her, and it's a dance-fever party all night long. Thanks for your guidance and support, Jen, which I desperately needed.

Nancy Yost, my agent since 1999, started her own company last year. I have every faith that the Nancy Yost Literary Agency will continue to be a huge success. As much faith as she's had in me over the years, I have in her tenfold. Congrats, Nancy!

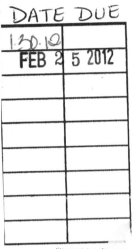